HERALDS AND HISTORY

Heralds and History

ROGER MILTON

DAVID & CHARLES

Newton Abbot . London . North Pomfret (Vt) . Vancouver

British Library Cataloguing in Publication Data

Milton, Roger
  Heralds and history.
  1. Heraldry - History
  I. Title
  929.6'09   CR151

  ISBN 0-7153-7475-3

Set in 11pt on 12pt Times
and printed in Great Britain
by Redwood Burn Limited, Trowbridge & Esher
for David & Charles (Publishers) Limited
Brunel House Newton Abbot Devon

Published in the United States of America
by David & Charles Inc
North Pomfret Vermont 05053 USA

Published in Canada
by Douglas David & Charles Limited
1875 Welch Street North Vancouver BC

Contents

Introduction

Over the past twenty years interest in heraldry has become much more widespread than used to be the case. One might almost add it has become fashionable. To the long line of distinguished writers ranging from Camden in the sixteenth century to Boutell in the late nineteenth there have been added in our own century already at least as many again who have produced authoritative works on various aspects of British heraldry. It surely follows that any new writer who is rash enough to enter these lists must do so with trepidation; and if he cannot claim to be either an armorist or a genealogist, in common decency he ought to preface his contribution with some sort of *apologia*. This I confess is more or less my own position, and because it seems to me that new disciples of this fascinating art and science are more likely to be recruited from the ranks of those whose reading taste is for the historical, my *apologia* is addressed to them.

In the first place I have to assume - I do not think it is too big an assumption - that the majority of these readers, having neither the time nor the opportunity for serious research, and reading mainly for pleasure and relaxation, tend to concentrate on the popular biography and historical novel. The standard of such writing today is remarkably high, most authors taking great pains to achieve historical accuracy; but in their survey of particular historical periods they are concerned mainly with those facts that are relevant to their particular themes. Among the phenomena of past ages generally omitted is the really extraordinary importance attached by almost all classes of medieval and renaissance society to heraldic blazoning and the compelling urge to secure an official grant of arms. The sober history textbooks, either through lack of space or because their authors consider the social, economic and political aspects so much more important, also fail to accord our subject its due place. As a schoolmaster whose job it has been to direct the reading of students I have been made very conscious of this omission. I have also discovered that many students, even young schoolboys have had their interest in heraldry whetted to a quite remarkable degree when they have been given a proper introduction to the subject. Therein lies the problem: to find suitable studies that place the subject fairly and squarely in its historical setting. The difficulty is that most books on heraldry tell the reader either not enough or too much.

The little books are naturally taken up with the work of explaining in a brief survey the more important rules and technical descriptions. In the big volumes the place in history tends to be obscured by the distinction they rightly make between *Amory* and *Heraldry*. The former term is applied to the study of the *science* of coat armour, that is description of the achievement, divisions of the shield, common charges and the marshalling of arms. Under the latter heading is included *all* matters relating to the heralds and their office. Absorbingly interesting though these classical works are to the advanced student, to the beginner they may present a problem calling for so much mental effort to master the intricate detail that he tends to lose sight of the larger aspect which is concerned equally with the place of heraldry in history. This book is the result of my attempt to combine the best of both worlds, to provide the beginner interested also in history with a simple but fairly comprehensive explanation of the science of Armory, and to set this firmly in its historical environment.

Finally I would like to express my appreciation of the help and advice I have received on a number of occasions from the College of Arms. I am especially grateful for the kindness of Dr Conrad Swan, York Herald of Arms, in agreeing to read the manuscript, and for all the valuable advice he has given me.

ROGER MILTON
November 1977

CHAPTER 1

Heralds and Heraldry

I

The symbols of heraldry confront the traveller all over Europe. On stone gatehouse, painted ceiling and carved overmantel, heraldic crest and shield bear silent witness to those family alliances and royal honours that gave birth to all those men and women who have left their mark on the pages of history. But heraldry is a living art: civic arms, regimental badges, school and college crests still proclaim the popularity and the importance of this ancient style of recording human achievement. With the departure of old European monarchies after World War I, most of the continental heraldic corporations have vanished for ever, but the College of Arms in England and the Court of the Lord Lyon King of Arms in Scotland receive many petitions for grants of arms from private citizens and from public corporations which include governments of the British Commonwealth and American states. It is also a fact that a very large number of private persons are prepared to pay considerable sums of money to have their ancestries traced in the hope that genealogical research will reveal that they are themselves entitled to bear ancient arms. Undoubtedly such armigerous activity lays the petitioners open to a charge of snobbery; nevertheless, the evidence that most have a genuine interest in historial antecedents seems overwhelming.

The truth is that heraldry presents not only a particularly fascinating and beautiful form of art, but also a valuable source of information for the student of history. Thus in the pages that follow an attempt is made not only to set down in as simple and as logical a way as possible explanations of the principal technical terms used by heralds together with the rules of emblazoning, but also to include references to the historical origins of many of the coats of arms belonging to famous persons which have been used by way of illustration. To these have been added historical explanations of the origins of many common devices painted on shields. However, before embarking on this course it is necessary to offer some explanation of the origins of the heralds themselves. For the purposes of this book, such explanation is confined to the history of the heralds in England.

II

It is not known exactly how the office of herald originated, but it seems probable that it developed out of the office of minstrel in the noble households of the early Middle Ages. At that period of Western European history the feudal barons were employing minstrels not only to provide entertainment in the form of song and verse as they sat at dinner or supper in their castle halls, but also as organisers of pageants and mock battles for the pleasure of visiting kings and other important persons. The royal household would of course have its own minstrels, and it is possible that the vastly greater amount of entertainment that had to be provided resulted in a division of labour, some minstrels being retained for the production of more traditional forms of entertainment, while others - perhaps the most intelligent - were deputed to devise pageants and to regulate the ceremonial for state occaions. If this was so, it would have been these latter minstrels who would have developed into the heralds of the thirteenth century. But it was the birth of the military tournament that gave them their real chance, and from the end of the thirteenth century we find these heralds accepting complete responsibility for the whole organisation of such martial displays.

In 1292 King Edward I laid it down in the famous Statue of Arms that 'neither kings of arms nor minstrels should carry hidden arms, nor any arms except pointless swords'. The same statute directed that they should wear their 'coat of arms', and from this livery came the familiar herald's tabard quartered back and front with the royal arms. No doubt in feudal times the heralds of the barons wore tabards blazoned with the arms of their lords, it being the universal custom for servants to wear on their livery their lord's badge.

With the end of the Wars of the Roses and the coming of the Tudor monarchs with their strong centralised government, the power of the feudal baron rapidly declined, and one consequence was that the feudal herald, finding his main occupation gone, gradually disappeared. But long before this the royal heralds had come to assume a position of unmatched responsibility and power, being in fact responsible for all grants of arms, the keeping of official records, and the organisation of state ceremonial. Moreover, from the end of the fourteenth century they had begun or organise themselves in degrees of rank under the supreme authority of the Lord High Constable of the Realm, though the position was not formalised until the issue of their first charter of incorporation in a college by King Richard III.

THE COLLEGE OF ARMS

Two years after the battle of Agincourt, that is in the year 1417, Thomas, Duke of Clarence, second son of King Henry IV and younger brother of Henry V, as Lord High Constable issued an order settling the order of precedence among the royal kings of arms and heralds, and it is from this time that the supreme authority of the Constable over the heralds can be said to date. At this time, too, emerged the three kings of arms who still guide the day-to-day activities of the heralds' college. Norroy King of Arms is first heard of at the end of the fourteenth century, and after 1417 his authority in matters heraldic north of the river Trent was generally recognised. By 1422 at the end of the reign of King Henry V Clarenceux King of Arms had become recognised as the chief herald responsible for the southern province, though holders of this office were to keep up an intermittent quarrel over the question of jurisdiction with Garter King of Arms until this matter was finally settled in the seventeenth century. It seems likely that his title came from his High Constable who was, as we have seen, Duke of Clarence.

Shortly before Agincourt Henry V revived the Order of the Garter, feeling no doubt that this revival of the first of the orders of chivalry would be in keeping with the noble concepts of medieval warfare that motivated the original founding in 1348 by King Edward III. In his revision of the Garter knights' constitution he made provision for a chief herald of the Order to be known under the title Garter King of Arms. Because of the importance attached to this revival, and the prestige attached to membership of the Companionship, this king of arms came rapidly to assume a position superior to that of the other two, and eventually achieved a position of *primus inter pares* among the three kings and so of great influence within the whole body of heralds. These claims did not, of course, pass unopposed, and in the sixteenth century when the rights of provincial visitations were much in evidence there was much bitter controversy, especially between the Garter and Clarenceux of the time. Provincial visitations were tours of inspection carried out at regular intervals by the kings of arms and attendant heralds to investigate the right of the gentry summoned by warrants of county sheriffs to bear arms. But the long reigns of the first two Garter Kings, William Bruges (1415-50) and John Smert (1450-78), who were both men of forceful character and considerable talent, did much to secure the office that degree of ascendancy it never afterwards lost.

Reference has been made to the fact that it was that much maligned monarch, King Richard III, who in 1483 gave the heralds their first charter incorporating them in a college with its headquarters at Coldharbour House in the City of London where they might keep their valuable records. Deprived of this home by the overthrow of the Plantagenet dynasty two years later, they were for the next seventy years without a headquarters; but the main provisions of King Richard's charter remained in force to be incorporated in the new charter issued under the authority of Queen Mary Tudor and her consort, King Phillip, on 18 July 1555. It is this charter that governs the College's existence today, and its chief points must be enumerated:

1 A record of all existing arms in the Realm was to be kept at the College.
2 No new arms to be displayed without the authority of the heralds.
3 New arms were to be granted only to those who could prove their status as gentlemen or who had by marriage entered the class of landed gentlemen.

These laws were incorporated from the original charter of 1483. To them were added certain others consequent upon the fourth Duke of Norfolk having been appointed Earl Marshal. It must be explained that when the Constable, Edward Stafford, Duke of Buckingham, was executed for high treason by Henry VIII in 1521 his authority over the heralds passed to his deputy, the Earl Marshal. The King, refusing to appoint another Constable, was content that the then Marshal, Charles Brandon, Duke of Suffolk, should have that authority. When he died the next Earl Marshal, Thomas Howard, third Duke of Norfolk, the Lord Treasurer, continued to exercise control, and so it has remained. Thomas, the fourth Duke, the son of the poet Earl of Surrey, was a cultured and enlightened nobleman whose influence on the future of the heralds' college was profound. It was largely his doing that Queen Mary and King Philip were persuaded to grant the new charter, and sixteen years later his famous Orders issued shortly before he became involved fatally in the Catholic Northern Rising set the seal on the continued existence of the College of Arms and its constitution.

The authority of the Earl Marshal over the College and its heralds was to be absolute. The number and titles of kings of arms, heralds and pursuivants in ordinary were to be as follows:

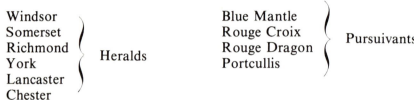

Garter Principal King of Arms
Clarenceux King of Arms (for the southern province)
Norroy King of Arms (for the northern province)

Windsor
Somerset
Richmond   Heralds
York
Lancaster
Chester

Blue Mantle
Rouge Croix
Rouge Dragon   Pursuivants
Portcullis

Garter's primacy over the other heralds was acknowledged, and in 1680 Henry Howard, Duke of Norfolk, as Earl Marshal decided that in the matter of official visitations by the heralds grants of arms were to be made by Garter and Clarenceux in the southern province and by Garter and Norroy in the northern province. The college was confirmed in its possession of Derby House, the headquarters granted by Mary and Philip in 1555. (The old Derby House was destroyed in the Great Fire of 1666, but most of the College's previous records were saved and are now housed in the present headquarters in Queen Victoria Street, a late seventeenth-century building occupying the original site.)

THE HERALDS AT WORK

It will be clear in the light of what has already been said that the main work of the heralds since the earliest times has been to keep records of existing arms, and to hold the responsibility for the granting and designing of all new arms. The practice of painting certain designs on the shields and banners of military knights had of course developed from the practical need to find an effective means of recognition in the confusion of battle where identical armour in the form of all-embracing chain mail was worn by friend and foe alike. To prevent duplication, therefore, was one of the earliest tasks of the heralds, and they sought to achieve this by reproducing in miniature on long parchment or vellum rolls the shields of lords and gentlemen, attested by brief written statements beneath each shield. Two of the oldest rolls of arms still in existence are treasured possessions of the College of Arms: Glover's Roll (named after the Elizabethan Somerset Herald whose researches brought it to the light of day), which dates from the year 1255 and contains some 250 shields; and the Great Roll which dates from c1254 and contains some 218 shields.

The increasing importance of the military tournament which called for the full panoply of heraldic blazoning, and above all the new code of chivalry inaugurated by King Edward III at the outset of the Hundred Years War, added enormously to the extent of the heralds' work. As the acknowledged authorities on armorial bearings these officers of arms jealously guarded their reputation, in particular being concerned not only to regulate exactly the designs of shields for new applicants, and the forms of 'difference' (addition to or change of tincture of original arms signifying family allegiance or junior membership of family) and 'augmentation' (addition made to original arms) made necessary following the practice of great lords of conferring on subordinates the right to bear some portion of their own arms; but also to concern themselves in the important matter of giving heraldic expression to the marriage of heirs in a predominantly feudal society.

These rules, which still largely obtain, form the subject matter of a large part of this book. The fact that so many of the words used in heraldic descriptions of arms are in French can be accounted for by recalling that Norman French was the language of court and polite society in England as well as in France at a time when these two ancient monarchies dominated Western Europe. It remains only to speak briefly of the two instruments at their disposal whereby the heralds at various periods of their history did their best to exercise control over an armigerous-minded society.

A series of regular visitations by the provincial kings of arms was begun in the reign of King Henry VIII, and continued down to the Revolution of 1688 when they ceased altogether. The new Tudor society included many men of the merchant and professional classes who were anxious to attain respectability as landed gentry. This was made possible after the Dissolution of the Monasteries by the purchase of monastic property; but a coat of arms was an essential adjunct, and it was largely to put a stop to unlawful adoption of arms by unscrupulous persons that the Earl Marshal of the day authorised the two kings of arms to conduct investigations at regular intervals in their respective provinces. Clarenceux in the south and Norroy in the north of England. The practice was for the king of arms accompanied by heralds and pursuivants to visit each hundred of a county where the sheriff had assembled the local gentry, and with the aid of the records he had brought with him to examine all claims to bear arms as well as petitions for new ones. Those found using arms to which they were not entitled were fined or in extreme cases imprisoned on the Earl Marshal's warrant. Grants for new arms had, as we have noted, to be approved also by Garter King of Arms. After visitations ceased in 1688 application for grants of new arms had to be made, as is still the case, through the College of Arms to the Earl Marshal for his warrant to the kings of arms for their granting Letters Patent of Arms under the seals and signs manual of Garter and a provincial King, or in certain cases all three Kings.

Known officially in the Middle Ages as 'Curia Militaris', the Court of Chivalry is generally believed to have come into existence c1347 when the Curia Regis or royal council delegated to the Constable and his deputy the Marshal power to settle disputes and hear cases 'touching deeds of arms and of war out of the realm, and also of things that touch arms or war within the realm, which cannot be discussed by the common law...' More than a hundred years before the College of Arms came into existence this Court settled such disputes, the High Constable and the Marshal presiding and deriving their authority from the royal prerogative. Even after visitations ceased, the Court, presided over now by the Earl Marshal alone, continued to be active, giving judgements in many prosecutions against persons charged with displaying arms without authority. In the year 1737 the Court of Chivlary sat for the last time for more than two hundred years under the Deputy Earl Marshal; the Dukes of Norfolk, as Catholics, were debarred under the terms of the Test Act of 1673 from acting officially. It was in fact not until the Catholic Emancipation Act of 1829 that it became possible for the Earl Marshal of the day to resume his functions, and not until 1954 that the penultimate holder of this office once more convened the Court to hear a complaint by Manchester City Corporation against a local cinema for displaying the city arms without permission. On this occasion as on earlier ones the heralds were present officially to offer their professional advice, and although the Court sat under the Lord Chief Justice acting by invitation as Surrogate in the Law Courts rather than in the Court of Chivalry at Derby House, the magnificent display of heraldic blazon, the Earl Marshal himself being present, must have recalled something of the splendours of an age long past.

The Court of Chivalry has not sat again, but the heralds of the College of Arms are perhaps as active as they have ever been, dealing with a stream of applications for grants of arms and researches into old pedigrees. To this work, of course, must be added their ceremonial duties, since they are in charge of all royal and state ceremony, and as such they have become in their gorgeous tabards familiar figures to the general public. It is perhaps worthy of note that the penultimate Earl Marshal, Bernard Marmaduke, sixteenth Duke of Norfolk, held the office for over fifty years, and presided over two coronations, the State Funeral of Sir Winston Churchill, the Investiture of the Prince of Wales at Carnarvon Castle, and was also responsible for the State funerals of Kings George V and George VI.

III

One of the pleasures to be derived from a study of heraldry is the ability to read in an achievement (complete display of crest, shield, supporters, mantling, motto) something of family history. When these arms belong to a family that had made its mark in history the result can be very rewarding. A good example dating from the fifteenth century is to be found in the arms of Richard Neville, Earl of Warwick, known to history as the 'King-Maker'. This great nobleman's wealth and political power were founded on a series of fortunate family marriages to heiress of great estates. The alienation of property was forbidden by law, with the result that a daughter inheriting brought the whole undivided family estate to her husband. Before enumerating and describing the Earl's quarterings (the division of the shield by lines into four or more sections) it will be as well to run briefly over the main events of his career.

He lived in that confused period of English history which was dominated by the Wars of the Roses. Supporting the house of York in its bid to supplant the weak, ineffective rule of Henry VI, this Neville earl eventually defeated the Lancastrian armies and secured the Crown for the Duke of York's son who ascended the throne in 1461 as King Edward IV. Giving himself over to a life of pleasure, the young king was for some years content to leave the government of the realm in the capable hands of his victorious general. But before long Edward began to show that he had a mind of his own. In defiance of Warwick, who he knew was negotiating a dynastic marriage with a French princess, he secretly married Elizabeth Woodville, an English commoner with many hanger-on relatives, and relations between the two men rapidly cooled. The King now assumed control of the government, and the Earl was sent to cool his heels as Governor of Calais where be brooded long over his master's 'ingratitude'. In the end he crossed to France and made his peace with his former enemy, Queen Margaret, the fierce consort of Henry VI. With French ships and a small body of troops provided by the French king, Louis XI, and leaving Queen Margaret and her son to follow with a larger force, Warwick returned to England to rouse the Lancastrians in a bid to restore the old king who was prisoner in the Tower. He was successful and King Edward was forced to flee into exile. But Warwick's triumph lasted less than a year, and on Easter Sunday, 1461, he was killed at the battle of Barnet fought between the Lancastrian army and a Yorkist army led by King Edward who had returned from exile to be acclaimed by Yorkist London. A month later the death of the Prince of Wales at the battles of Tewkesbury not only put an end to Lancastrian hopes, but finally extinguished the old feudal power which the King-Maker had done his best to prolong.

The table of descent of Richard Neville should be read and compared with

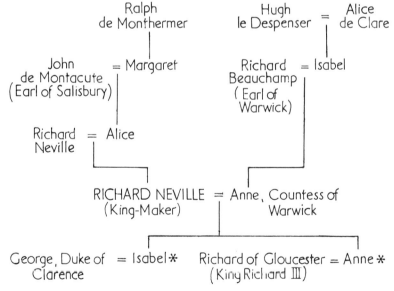

*These daughters were the Neville heirs. Isabel, the elder, married George Duke of Clarence, heir presumptive of King Edward IV; while Anne, the younger daughter, married the Duke of Gloucester, the future King Richard III. It was a quarrel over the inheritance of the great earl's estates that contributed to Clarence's execution for treason, drowned, it is said, in a butt of Malmsey wine in the Tower. Edward IV had decreed that the inheritance should be divided equally between the two daughters, Clarence's

son, Edward, Earl of Warwick, debarred from the succession by the act of attainder that condemned his father, suffered judicial murder by Henry VII in 1499, while his sister Margaret, Countess of Salisbury, was executed as late as 1541 by orders of Henry VIII, ostensibly because her royal Plantagenet blood constituted a threat to the Tudor dynasty. Her son, Reginald Cardinal Pole, the great-grandson of the King-Maker, lived to become the last Catholic Archbishop of Canterbury.

the arms of the Earl (Fig 1). It becomes clear how, inheriting through the female line from the Montacutes and from the Beauchamps respectively, he became Earl of Salisbury and Earl of Warwick. To this concentration of territorial and military strength, it will be seen, was added inheritance from the rich and powerful families of Despenser and Clare. To the feudal knights and squires trained from boyhood to read armorial bearings, the sight of the great earl's banners with their proud claims fluttering aloft must have given both confidence and inspiration.

The heraldic language used to describe the arms of the Earl of Warwick (opposite) is explained in the pages that follow. The Warwick arms should be studied again when these pages have been assimilated. Figs 20-28 show the hatchings used in heraldry to indicate metal, colour and fur in black and white representations.

1 — **Beauchamp:**	Gules, a fess or between 6 cross crosslets or
2 — **Montacute:**	Argent, 3 fusils fesswise gules
3 — **Monthermer:**	Or, and eagle displayed vert
4 — **Warwick:**	Checky or and azure, a chevron ermine
5 — **Neville:**	Gules, a saltire argent with a label gobony argent and azure (the label shows that Anne Neville inherited the Warwick arms as a junior member of that family)
6 — **Clare:**	Or, 3 chevronels gules
7 — **Despenser:**	Quarterly argent and gules fretty or, over all a bend sable.

CHAPTER 2

The Achievement

Achievement is really a collective noun which has been employed to describe an assembly of those parts of a medieval knight's equipment that can be displayed in an heraldic blazon. These, which are seven in number, are listed in Figure 2.

1—Crest
2—Wreath (sometimes called the Torse)
3—Helmet (or Helm in eighteenth-century terminology)
4—Shield (called Escutcheon in old heraldry)
5—Supporters (restricted to certain classes)
6—Motto (usually displayed at foot or above crest)
7—Mantling

2

    Items 1, 3, 4 and 7 represent actual items of battle equipment, while items 2, 5 and 6 are to be regarded as accessories. Item 4, the shield, is the most important because on its wide, flat surface are always emblazoned the particular arms of the owner of the achievement. Much of this book must necessarily be devoted to explanations of the divisions, tinctures, and charges which find their place thereon: but before we can do this it is necessary to explain the origin and the purpose of all seven items (Fig 2).

1   The Crest

In vulgar parlance the word crest is often used indiscriminately to describe the crest proper, the blazoned arms or both together. In heraldry it always refers to the appendage fixed to the top of the helmet. In the Middle Ages knightly crests were fashioned in the style of animals, birds, and a variety of inanimate objects. They were made of wood or leather boiled to make it hard, and were originally designed to provide additional protection for the head against blows from battle-axe or sword. One of the first recorded appearances seems to have been that adopted by Edmund Crouchback, Earl of Lancaster and younger brother of King Edward I (1272-1307). During the course of the fourteenth century the use of crests became more general, and at the same time they became more decorative. No doubt the increasing importance of the knightly tournament, where jousting warriors might be expected to arm themselves with their finest equipment, had much to do with this new popularity. In the middle of the century that paladin of knightly chivalry, King Edward III (1327-1377), adopted the lion which has remained the royal crest ever since. The illustrations on later pages will show an extraordinary variety of objects that have been chosen as crests. One peer, for example, adopted a bucket and chain.

The usual position of the crest in achievements is at the top; but there are many examples, usually in family tombs, of its being displayed at the feet of the recumbent effigy. It is, however, always found attached to the helmet.

2   The Wreath

This item represents a piece of twisted cloth used to hide the attachment of the crest to the helmet. The wreath is usually emblazoned in the two principal colours of the main blazon. The fashion was introduced in the fourteenth century.

An alternative custom introduced more or less at the same time was to encircle the crest near its join with the helmet with a crown or coronet (not a coronet of rank), or by a cap of estate which rested on the helmet. The cap was usually tinctured red with a turned-up ermine brim.

3   The Helmet

This head defence worn by the armoured knight in battle and in tournament must not be confused with the balaclava-like head covering which until the fifteenth century was always worn under the battle helmet as part of the all-embracing chain mail. The confusion may have arisen because many ancient brasses and memorials show warriors so clad; but their helmets are in fact usually depicted lying at their feet. The helmet was a cumbersome item of armour put on at the last minute before joining battle or commencing a joust.

The shape and style of the helmet have varied considerably down the centuries from the conical domed type with nose guard of the Conqueror's time which left the face entirely exposed, to the complicated, completely enclosing snout and bascinet types of the fifteenth century. Seven forms of helmet are illustrated in Figs 3-13. It is usually the armet and bascinet that are emblazoned in heraldry, shown in profile to present to best advantage the crest, which on the helmet would naturally be facing front. Exceptions to this custom are given in the next paragraph.

Eleventh-century Norman helmet with *nasal* (Fig 3)
Twelfth-century (Richard I) (Fig 4)
Thirteenth-century (Fig 5)
Early type of bascinet (early thirteenth century) (Fig 6)
Fourteenth-century bascinet (Fig 7)
Early fifteenth-century 'snout' type (Fig 8)
Late fifteenth-century jousting helmet (Fig 9)
Fifteenth-century sallad (salade) (Fig 10)
Late fifteenth-century armet (Fig 11)
Sixteenth-century English Closed helmet (Fig 12)
Late fifteenth-century 'grilled' helmet (buckler) (Fig 13). This

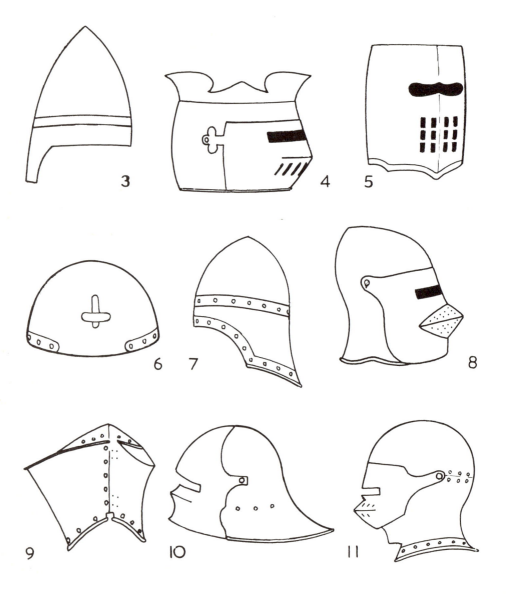

pageant helmet was borne in the funeral procession of the Holy Roman Emperor Frederic III (1493). This emperor, who was the father of the emperor Maximilian and the great-grandfather of the emperor Charles V, was the last of a long line to receive the imperial crown from the Pope in a coronation in Rome.

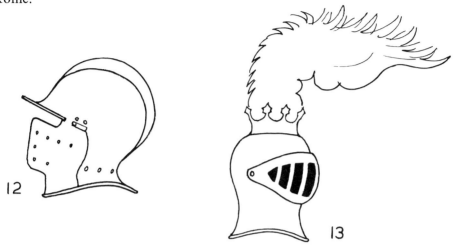

In post-medieval heraldry the custom arose of displaying different types of helmet in achievements to indicate the rank of the owner. In such cases the facing direction also varied according to rank:

> Kings and royal princes: gold helmet, facing front,
>   6-7 gold bars in visor
> Peers of the realm: steel helmet facing three-quarters
>   left, 5 gold bars in visor
> Knight or baronet: steel helmet facing front,
>   solid visor displayed open
> Esquire (gentleman): steel helmet facing left,
>   closed visor

4 The Shield

This was the chief defensive weapon borne in battle and in tournaments by all mounted knights and esquires. Its shape has varied considerably down the centuries, as shown in Figs 14–18:

> In early Norman times (eleventh century)
>   it was 'kite-shaped' (Fig 14)
> By the end of the twelfth century it had become
>   an elongated triangle (Fig 15)
> By the middle of the fourteenth century it had
>   become convex, because it had been discovered
>   that offensive weapons tended to glance off the
>   curved surface (Fig 16)

By the end of the fourteenth century a further
development had brought the four-sided shield
with a point on the base side (Fig 17)
In the fifteenth century came the final development:
a notch in the top dexter (right) corner to act as a
lance rest. This type of shield may have been used
in tournaments only (Fig 18)

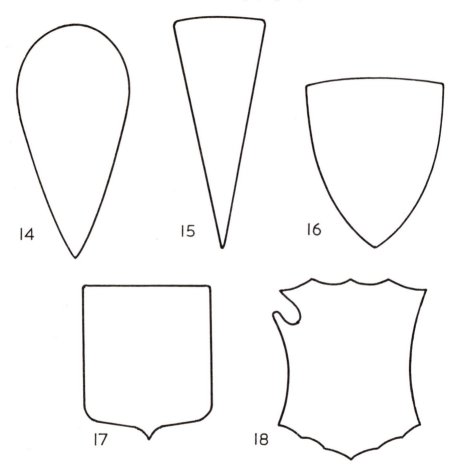

5   The Supporters

This is the name given to the animals, mythical beasts, birds or humans who 'support' the shield, one on either side. Supporters do not figure in the earliest recorded arms. Their origins are to be found in the thirteenth century on seals. The systematic use of supporters of the shield emerges in the mid-fifteenth century. It has been suggested that the invention was born of the engraver's need to fill up on his round seal the spaces left vacant after he had sculpted the square shield, and this is borne out by such evidence as is available. One of the earliest seals that includes supporters is that of Edmund Crouchback (see above) whose engraved shield is flanked by two wyverns. A hundred years later the private seal of Henry Bolingbroke, Duke of Lancaster, was to bear two swans, while after he became King Henry IV (1399-1413) two antelopes flanked the shield of his Queen, Mary de Bohun. The fashion catching on, it was a small step to emblazoning supporters in general achievements. It was not until the end of the sixteenth century that some attempt was made to restrict this privilege to persons of high rank. In modern times the right to include supporters in their arms is granted to Knights Grand Cross (or their equivalent) of the senior orders of chivalry, and to a few privileged commoners, including Companions of the Order of Canada as well as Canadian Governors General and Lieutenant Governors. It should be noted that there is nothing in the rules to say that both supporters must be identical: the Lion and the Unicorn of the British royal arms are a case in point.

6   The Motto

The words of the motto are generally emblazoned on an open scroll placed at the base of the shield; but it may be placed in some other position, as, for example, when the achievement forms part of the embellishment of a tomb. The form of words, which may be Latin, French, German or English, nearly always refers to some dramatic event in the life of the founder or another closely related member of the family. Mottoes often spring from scriptural or proverbial sources, for example, 'Loyalti Me Ly' (Loyalty binds me), the personal motto of King Richard III; or 'Fortiter Triumphans Defendit' (Triumphing by brave defence), motto of Newcastle-upon-Tyne, which although the reference is to a courageous defence of the town during the Civil War of 1644 might equally well refer to the town's importance in defence since Roman times. The motto of the Prince of Wales, 'Ich Dien', may have been adopted first by the Black Prince as a tribute to the brace old blind King of Bohemia who was killed fighting at Crécy in 1346. Certainly this Prince of Wales adopted as his 'shield of peace' the three ostrich feathers which have become also the badge of the heir to the throne who, usually being the Prince of Wales, finds that his badge is commonly described as the 'Prince of Wales' Feathers'. No one really knows the true origin of mottoes. A possible explanation is that they came from the war cries of tribal chiefs and feudal lords leading their men into battle.

7   The Mantling

From the end of the fourteenth century it became the custom for emblazoners to cover the coronet or cap of estate encircling the crest with the representation of a scarf or cloth hanging behind. By the second half of the fifteenth century this cloth had not only become more ornamental and much larger, but now extended down both sides of the helmet and part of the shield in a series of graceful twists to form a graceful pattern with the rest of the achievement. The usual colour of this mantling was red with a lining exposed of ermine fur; but there were no fixed rules, many examples being found of other tinctures— silver, gold, blue, black, checky, etc. Opinion is divided on the question of origin. Some authorities believe it stems from the knight's 'mantle' which, copying the Saracens, he wore in Crusading times over his armour in the Holy Land to prevent it getting too hot in the eastern sun. Others link the mantling with the houseling cloth with which it became the fashion to deck the destrier or war horse for tournaments. As this latter custom does not appear to have been adopted until the fifteenth century, it would seem more likely that the first explanation is the true one.

One more item remains to be described: the Compartment. This is the base on which the achievement sometimes stands, and is not part of the achievement itself. The compartment of the royal arms is a green field in which grow the floral emblems of England, Scotland, Ireland and Wales.

CHAPTER 3

Tinctures, Partitions, Ordinaries and Sub-Ordinaries

We are now in a position to begin our study of the principal item of the achievement, that is, the shield. No doubt the art of reading correctly a complicated escutcheon such as the Warwick arms at first sight appears to present considerable difficulty. Nevertheless, careful study of the rules and definitions and the sketches and diagrams in the pages that follow ought to reveal the logical simplicity of the heralds' art.

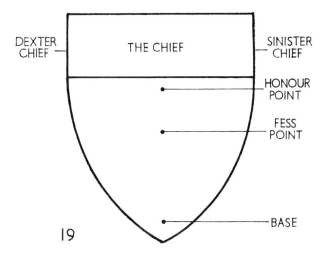

We should begin by taking a further look at the shield itself. This is, in a manner of speaking, the blank canvas of the heraldic painter. Fig 19 shows the following features:

> *Dexter* meaning right, and *Sinister* meaning left are always given from the point of view of the knight holding the shield, that is in reverse as we look from the front.
> The *Chief* is the whole area above a partition line drawn across the shield about one-third down. This area is frequently painted in different colours from those employed for the rest of the shield. The Chief often bears its own charges.
> The *Honour Point,* which marks the position on which in certain circumstances a charge is placed, was originally the point on the shield aimed at by the knight in a joust.
> The *Fess Point* marks the exact centre of the shield on the horizontal partition line known as the *Fess* (see *Ordinaries*).
> The *Base* is the area of the apex of the shield, and the lowest section when it is held in its normal position.

Tinctures

Colours in heraldry are known as 'tinctures'. With certain furs and metals commonly used for emblazoning, which are also called tinctures, these number thirteen. These are divided into groups:

Colours: Azure (blue)
               Gules (red)
               Sable (black)
               Vert (green)
               Purpure (purple)
               Murrey or Sanguine (blood red)
               Tenné (orange)
Metals: Or (gold)
               Argent (silver)
Furs: Ermine (black ermine tails on silver ground)
               Ermines (white ermine spots on black ground)
               Erminois (black ermine spots on gold ground)
               Vair (alternate pattern of blue and silver cup-shaped figures to
                  represent fur marking of the blue-grey squirrel)

For illustrations of arms printed in black and white, the heralds indicate particular colour, metal or fur by distinctive shading known as 'hatching'. Hatching of more common tinctures is illustrated in Figs 20-28.

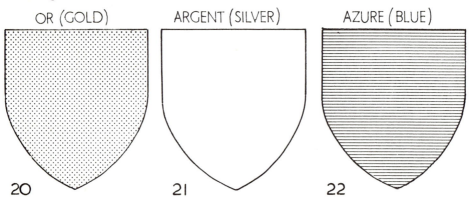

There is no rule as regards the particular shade of colours, and some variation is possible. The tinctures Murrey and Tenne are comparatively rare. The use of fur for emblazoning stems from the fact that in the Middle Ages the employment of this material for clothing was graded according to rank, the rarer and more costly furs being restricted to persons of high degree. Thus, ermine was confined to royal princes, miniver to noblemen and royal judges, squirrel to knights and wealthy merchants. It must be remembered that fur had an extremely practical use for medieval people living in cold and draughty stone halls and castles.

The Rules of Tincture state that a metal may not be painted on a metal, a fur may not be painted on a fur and a colour may not be painted on a colour. A charge on a shield, or as any other part of the achievement, being human, animal, bird, flower, or well-known object, may be emblazoned in its natural colours. It is then described as being *proper*.

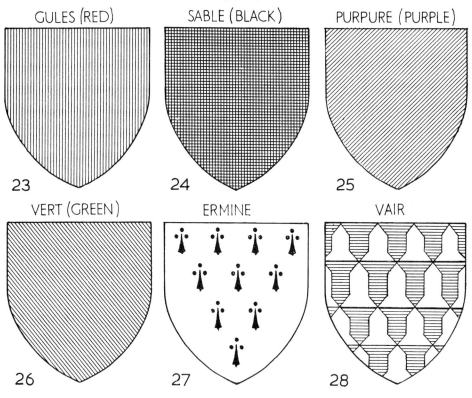

Partition Lines and Ordinaries

Partition lines are the lines by which a shield may be divided for the purpose of emblazoning in different tinctures. They vary both in direction and in pattern, and they have been given exact names (Figs 29-37).

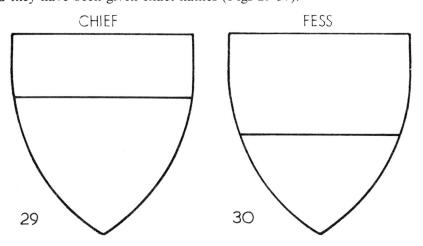

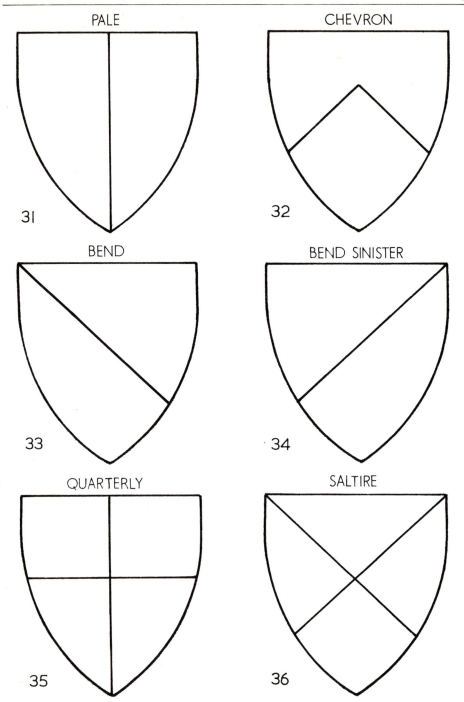

PALE

CHEVRON

31

32

BEND

BEND SINISTER

33

34

QUARTERLY

SALTIRE

35

36

Where partition lines or ordinaries are mentioned without any qualification they are always straight lines, as in the examples given in Figs 29-37. When these lines are not straight they are classified as patterns under titles as shown in Figs 38-43.

PILE

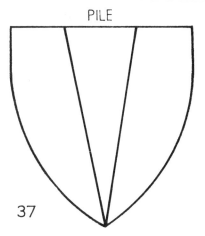

37

CHIEF INDENTED

38

CROSS ENGRAILED

39

BORDER INVECTED

40

FESS EMBATTLED

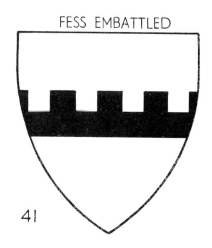

41

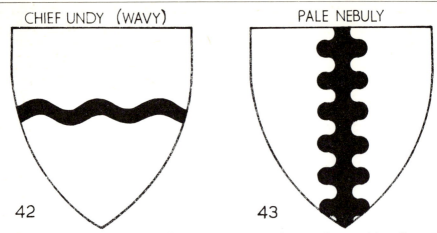

CHIEF UNDY (WAVY)

PALE NEBULY

42

43

The ordinaries are of great importance. They follow the partition lines, but differ by being broad bands which are given distinctive tinctures. They often bear charges of their own. It is believed that originally they represented the fastenings of the war shield, and at a later date were converted into ornaments by painting. The principal ordinaries are shown in Figs 44–53.

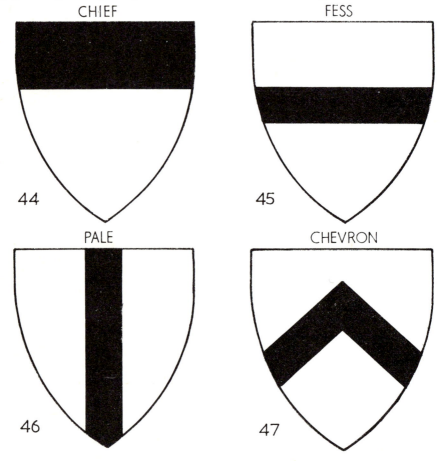

CHIEF

FESS

44

45

PALE

CHEVRON

46

47

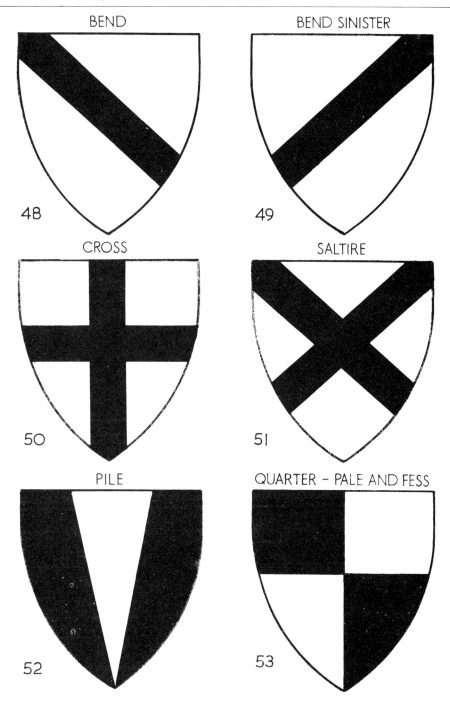

BEND

BEND SINISTER

48

49

CROSS

SALTIRE

50

51

PILE

QUARTER – PALE AND FESS

52

53

Multiples of certain of the ordinaries frequently occur, and these have their own names. The examples in Figs 54-61 show how these multiple ordinaries may be recognised. They are usually emblazoned in two tinctures, one being of the field.

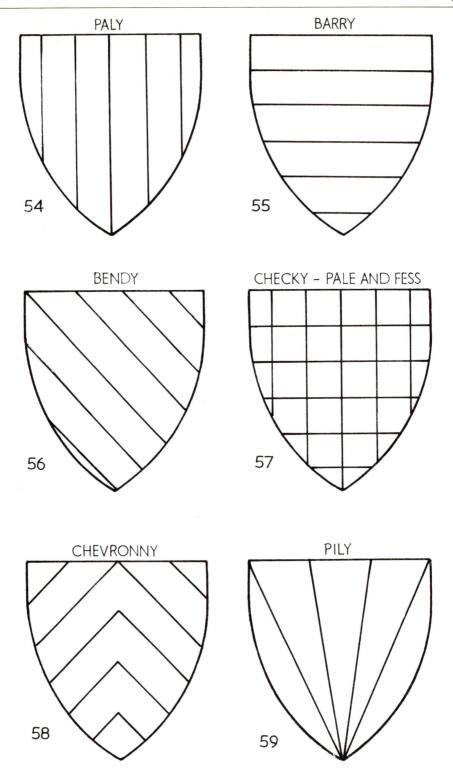

PALY

BARRY

54

55

BENDY

CHECKY – PALE AND FESS

56

57

CHEVRONNY

PILY

58

59

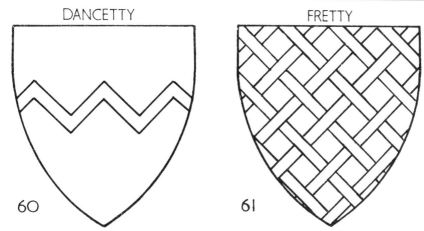

Two multiple ordinaries which are not, strictly speaking, variations of principal ordinaries are shown in Figs 62-63.

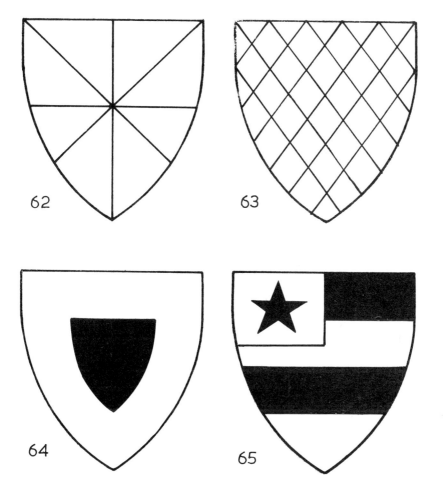

66   67

SUB-ORDINARIES

There are a number of objects and geometric figures in common use that may be considered under this heading. Some of them are further variations of ordinaries, while others more nearly approximate to charges (see Chapter 4).

Inescutcheon (Shield of Pretence) The placing of a smaller shield upon a larger. When it contains the arms of a man's wife it signifies that she is an heraldic heir, that is to say she has no brothers or they and their issue have all died so that she represents her male-line family. (Fig 64)

Canton A shield of pretence occupying the dexter quarter in chief. Augmentations are quite often borne in this way. On other occasions the canton is used to identify certain types of heraldic heirship and representation, such as when the heraldic heir was heir to her mother but not to her father. (Fig 65)

Bordure (Border) This is what its name suggests. The bordure may bear charges of its own, and often has a different tincture. (Fig 66)

Orle A bordure which does not reach the edges of the shield at any point. In early times the orle was used as a mark of difference (see Chapter 6). (Fig 67)

68   69

Tressure A narrow orle set *within* the shield and usually decorated with heraldic flowers, such as the lily. This sub-ordinary is almost always found as a double tressure, as in the royal Scottish arms illustrated, where lilies are placed alternately upper and lower half of the flower both sides of the tressure. (Fig 68)

Gyron The geometrical figure formed when the shield is divided per fess, per pale, per bend and per bend sinister. (Fig 69)

Lozenge A square set diagonally like a playing-card diamond. The lozenge is seldom found as a single charge, but in pale or in fess.

Fusil This is an elongated lozenge. Fusils in line together are often emblazoned in the form of chevron, bend or fess. (Fig 71)

Mascle Technically known as a voided lozenge, the mascle is simply a lozenge with the centre cut out. (Fig 72)

Roundel This is a round disc seldom emblazoned singly. When it forms a charge in numbers on a shield, the roundel is given other names according to the particular tincture, which there is then no need to name separately:

Colour	Name of roundel
Or	Bezant
Argent	Plate
Azure	Hurt
Gules	Torteau
Sable	Pellet
Vert	Pompey
Purpure	Golpe

Crescent Usually emblazoned with the horns of the crescent uppermost. This sub-ordinary is often charged as a mark of cadency (see Chapter 6).(Fig 73)

Molet or Mullet This is really a five-pointed star. It is often emblazoned with a hole in the centre, when it is correctly to be described as a 'pierced molet'. Like the lozenge and the roundel, the molet is seldom found singly. (Fig 74)

Annulet A double circle tintured to form a ring. It is seldom emblazoned singly, but when it is it is a mark of cadency (Chapter 6). (Fig 75)

Flanches These are two curved segments of the shield on either side, dexter and sinister. They bear a tincture different from that of the field. (Fig 76)

72   73

74   75

76   77

Cinquefoil This object might be classed under common charges (Chapter 4) since it is a representation of a five-branched leaf. The cinquefoil, however, is often tinctured in metals and other colours than green. When this particular form has three leaves it is named a 'trefoil', and when it has four a 'quatrefoil'. (Fig 77)

Billet This is a small rectangular object resembling a brick but not showing perspective. It may be tinctured in any colour or metal. When the shield is charged with a number of billets not being in fess, pale, or any other particular

formation, it is to be described as 'billety'. (Fig 78)

Cross Heraldry being a product of the medieval Christian world, it is entirely in keeping with the spirit of that age that the supreme Christian symbol should figure prominently in the arms of many knights and Christian institutions. The white cross of the Knights Hospitaller of St John of Jerusalem and the red cross of St George adopted by the Crusaders to be worn as badges on mantle and surcoat must have provided noblemen with a powerful incentive to incorporate in one form or another in their arms the 'sign' by which the Emperor Constantine conquered the world for Christ. The plain Greek cross with head, feet and arms extending to the edge of the shield has been illustrated as a principal ordinary because it is in effect a combination of pale and fess. A number of heraldic variations, listed as sub-ordinaries are shown in Figs 79-89:

Cross Couped (Greek Cross) (Fig 79)
Cross of Calvary (Fig 80)
Cross Moline (Fig 81)
Cross Bottonny (Fig 82)
Cross Patonce (Fig 83)
Cross Patée (Fig 84)
Cross Crosslet (Fig 85)
Cross Potent (Fig 86)
Cross of Andrew (Saltire) (Fig 87)
Cross Quarterly (Pierced) (Fig 88)
Cross Fitchy (Fig 89)

Any form of the cross that has the foot pointed is known as a cross fitchy. The most common is the plain Greek cross, closely followed by the cross patee. The cross fitchy sable still appears on the arms of the archbishops of Canterbury (see Chapter 9). When the field of a shield is charged with a number of crosslets scattered in no special formation, it should be described as 'crusilé' or 'crusily'.

CHAPTER 4
Common Charges

From the earliest times of the history of heraldry there has been a remarkable variety of *charges* placed on shields and emblazoned on crests. Often, but not always, these have either perpetuated the memory of some exploit or incident in the early history of the owner's family, or have been symbolic of the profession of the founder. In modern times the latter is more likely to be the case; and, as we shall note, there are a number of cases in which such charges have a punning reference to the name or title of the owner.

This chapter is concerned with the heraldic descriptions of the more common charges, together with brief accounts of their historic origins and symbolism. As a matter of convenience we may group them under the following natural divisions: Human; Mythical Beasts; Animals; Birds; Fish; Flowers and Other Plants; Celestial Objects; Other Inanimate Objects.

HUMAN CHARGES

In the Christian Europe of an earlier age it might be expected that figures of saints and even of the Deity would occur frequently in heraldry. Actually this has not been so, the medieval heralds apparently preferring to emblazon some relic or article closely associated with a particular saint (eg St Andrew's cross)

90

91

The sculpted figures of Christ and the saints seen carved in and outside cathedrals, monasteries and churches are of course representative of devotional art and not heraldic at all. One of the few examples of the Deity as a heraldic charge is to be found in the arms of the English see of Chichester which shows God the Father enthroned in splendour giving the episcopal blessing with the two first fingers of the dexter hand. The see of Salisbury bears 'Azure, the Virgin and Child or'. Classical and allegorical figures appear more frequently (eg the figure of Neptune in the arms of a former Lancaster Herald, and the arms of the University of Melbourne which include the figure of

Victory, 'robed and attired proper'). Cherubs are more frequently met with, usually depicted as a child's head between two wings displayed.

The whole human figure more frequently appears as supporters and in crests rather than as shield charges (but see Fig 90). However, emblazoned attitude, costume and actions should be described, eg 'Sable, a naked man, his arms extended proper'. Sometimes the upper half only of the human form is emblazoned, usually 'issuing from' a crown or other object in a crest. It must then be described as a 'demi-man' or 'demi-lady'. Commonly found are certain portions of the human anatomy such as head, arm, leg and hand. In these cases certain rules will apply to describe race, position, action, etc, and these rules are set forth among the rules of blazon in Chapter 5.

MYTHICAL BEASTS

Legends abounded in the Middle Ages of the activities of these strange creatures, and frequently appeared in the literature of the time. No doubt it was natural for a people limited in their travels by the primitive means at their disposal - except in times of emergency, the average man hardly left his own village, and sailors in their tiny ships seldom ventured beyond known coastal waters - to imagine distant unknown territories and seas peopled by fabulous monsters. It was the fear of such creatures that made it so difficult for Columbus to find crews for the ships of his first voyage of discovery, and even educated persons believed in the fabulous creatures described in Sir John Mandeville's famous book. It was, then, entirely natural that many of these creatures from classical and medieval legend should find their way into the emblazoner's art.

The Dragon This four-legged creature is usually depicted breathing out flames. In holy scripture associated with Satan and the war in heaven against St Michael and the angels of God, the dragon, we are told, was cast out on the earth to work havoc among the children of men 'for a season'. Long before Spenser wrote *The Faerie Queene* the dragon was matched against St George, who represents Christian man battling against evil. St George was adopted as their patron by the Crusaders after, as the anonymous author of the contemporary account of the First Crusade wrote, the Saint appeared before the walls of Antioch with a company of celestial warriors on white horses to rout the horde of Turkish warriers advancing on the besieged Christians. It was doubtless the devotion of English knights to this saint ever since their ancestors fought under Richard Coeur de Lion in the Third Crusade that played an important part in the adoption of St George as the principal patron of England in the middle of the fourteenth century. To this day his festival is celebrated on 23 April, and St George vanquishing the Dragon forms the motif of the 'George' suspended from the gold collar of the Most Noble Order of the Garter. (Fig 91)

The Gryphon Sometimes called 'Griffin', this was a four-legged dragon-like creature, but with the head, chest, claws and wings of an eagle. The hind part and tail were those of a lion. In more modern times Lewis Carroll has given this creature a more kindly nature than that of legend was supposed to possess. (Fig 92)

The Wyvern This was, according to legend, a two-legged creature with webbed wings like the Gryphon, but with eagles's claws and feet, eagle's head, and a long but barbed and knotted tail. (Fig 93)

The Unicorn A graceful, white-skinned animal with a long and slender single horn rising from its brow. Legend has it that this beautiful creature was visible only to virgins and to the pure in heart. Many poets, including Spenser, have written of this magical creature. The unicorn, of course, forms one of the two supporters of the royal arms. (Fig 94)

The Salamander A scaly creature like a large lizard which was supposed to live by eating fire. In legend the salamander actually inhabits regions of natural fire like volcanoes. One of Algernon Blackwood's finest stories of the macabre is concerned with these creatures. It is emblazoned with flames issuing from its mouth. (Fig 95)

The Sea Hart An antlered stag, but in place of legs the creature has a fish tail. Like the heraldic sea horse and the sea lion and, of course, the mermaid, the sea hart is the product of an age when the vast ocean, then unknown to sailors who seldom took their little ships out of sight of land, was supposed to be peopled by many unknown and terrifying magical creatures. Perhaps some substance may be given to legend by comparison with actual sea lions and sea horses known to fishermen. (Fig 96)

The Martlet A bird not unlike a swallow (hirondelle), but with no legs. The martlet is a very common charge. (Fig 97)

ANIMALS

The very great variety of species of animal that have been emblazoned as crests, charges on shields, and supporters makes it impossible to do more than describe and illustrate a few of the more popular.

The Lion Perhaps because of its noble appearance and ancient title, 'King of the Beasts', emperors and kings were delighted to have the designation 'Lion' bestowed upon them. As early as 1127 the Norman King Henry I (1100-1135) sent his son-in-law, the Holy Roman Emperor Henry V, a shield charged with a lion. After the Emperor's death his widow married Geoffrey, Count of Anjou, who became the father of the first English Plantagenet monarch, Henry

II (1154-1189). This great king seems to have adopted as his royal arms the shield of his mother's first husband, the Emperor, but it was his own son, Richard I, Coeur de Lion, who added two more lions to make the royal arms of England what they have ever since remained: 'gules, three lions, passant regardant or'. (In the early Middle Ages the heraldic lion, when emblazoned in any position other than 'rampant', was referred to as a leopard. One possible explanation is that in those days few people in northern Europe, including heralds, knew the difference between a lion and a leopard.) (Fig 98)

The Stag (Hart) To hunt this beast in the extensive forests of medieval England was the prerogative of the king and the feudal nobility. No doubt the privilege was so jealously guarded - the penalties for poaching were formidable - because after the November slaughtering of cattle for lack of winter feed venison remained one of the very few meats of quality available for castle hall until summer. The head alone is usually charged on shields, but the whole animal appears as a crest or supporter. The white hart was the personal cognizance of King Richard II (1377-1399) and so appeared on his arms. (Fig 99)

The Boar This beast, frequently referred to by its French name of *sanglier,* was, after the stag, the principal animal of the chase hunted by king and Norman baron: and thus quite naturally became a popular charge on medieval arms, though the head alone was customarily emblazoned. The boar was the principal charge on the personal arms of King Richard III (1483-1485), and the Lancastrian opponents of the last of the Plantagenets made political capital out of this by a piece of contemporary doggerel verse:

> The Cat, the Rat, and Lovell the Dog
> Ruled all England under the Hog.

Sir William Catesby, Sir Richard Ratcliffe and Francis, Lord Lovell, were ministers of King Richard, who was, of course, 'the Hog'. In medieval and Tudor times the boar's head roasted and garnished with gelatine and other confections formed the *pièce de résistance* at great feasts, especially that of Christmas when it was carried in procession into the banqueting hall, often to the accompaniment of trumpet and drum music. This ancient custom is still followed on Christmas Day at The Queen's College, Oxford, when the 'Boar's Head' carol is sung by the College Choristers and the procession advances to the high table where the Provost and Fellows are seated. (Fig 100)

The Wolf A symbol of ferocity, this beast, usually the head only, but showing fangs and tongue with a different tincture, appears on some early shields. According to legend, the last wolf in English forests was hunted down and killed some time in the reign of King Edward IV (1461-1483), while the wolf survived in Scotland until the eighteenth century. (Fig 101)

The Hare Though a less important animal of the chase, the hare often appeared on the menu of those gargantuan medieval feasts of three courses where a single course consisted of many different kinds of meat, birds and confections. In heraldry the animal is customarily emblazoned 'courant' (running). (Fig 102)

The hart, the boar, the wolf and the hare are known as the four heraldic Beasts of Venery (animals for royal hunts).

102

103

104

105

The Bull A bold and fierce animal, the bull was ever regarded by medieval knighthood as a suitable object of emblazoning, either as charge or as crest. More usually the head only has been charged, and readers of *Ivanhoe* will remember that a bull's head formed the principal charge of that fierce Norman knight, Sir Reginald Front de Boeuf, though at the time in which Scott set his novel it is doubtful whether full arms were being granted by heralds. A fine example of the whole animal as a supporter is to be found in the achievement of the county of Devon which has as dexter supporter a Devon bull. (Fig 103)

The Bear The popularity of the bear in heraldry is attested by the frequency of its appearance on English inn signs. Especially is this the case in

Warwickshire where the 'bear and ragged staff' are emblazoned as a principal charge on the county arms. The origin of this lies with the Beauchamp Earls of Warwick who from the mid-thirteenth century used bear and staff as separate emblems of their personal arms. In the mid-fifteenth century when Richard Neville, the King-Maker, inherited the Warwick earldom he combined these two emblems which thereafter remained a principal charge of his achievement. One hundred years later when Robert Dudley inherited Kenilworth Castle, the ancestral home of the Earls of Warwick, he made frequent use of the 'bear and ragged staff', both as a personal emblem and as a badge of livery. It must be borne in mind that although Queen Elizabeth had created him Earl of Leicester, he was a younger son of that Earl of Warwick who had been a minister of Henry VIII and had finally as Duke of Northumberland suffered execution for high treason at the beginning of the reign of Mary Tudor. Why the Beauchamp earls should have adopted this animal as a device is unknown. It is possible that the association of the beast with the quality of rugged strength had something to do with it. It must not be forgotten, too, that throughout the Middle Ages and for long after a very popular English entertainment was to match the cunning of a mastiff against the brute strength of a bear. (Fig 104)

The Lamb Because of its association with the Bible and with Greek myth, the lamb and its fleece have frequently been subjects for blazon. The Paschal Lamb, symbol of the risen Christ, was adopted as their special emblem by the Order of Knights Templar. Many religious houses in the Middle Ages adopted this animal in various forms, and in the middle of the fifteenth century Philip the Good, Duke of Burgundy, chose a golden fleece as the principal item of insignia for his new order of chivalry, the *Toisson D'Or*. No doubt as a great renaissance prince he had in mind the Greek legend of Jason and the Argonauts. The fact remains that for nearly five hundred years the Order of the Golden Fleece was to remain the most coveted in western Europe. On the death in battle in 1477 of Charles the Rash, the last of the independent dukes of Burgundy, the sovereignty of the Order passed to Philip of Hapsburg, son of the Emperor Maxmilian and Duke Charles's heir, Mary. From Philip it passed to his own son, the Emperor Charles V, and the Holy Roman and Austrian emperors continued to award this much coveted decoration right down to 1918 when the imperial Hapsburg line came to an end with the abdication of the Emperor Charles. It so happened also that by an earlier abdication, the voluntary one of the great Charles V himself who was also King of Spain, what many considered the legal sovereignty of the Golden Fleece passed to Charles's son who now became Philip II of Spain and as ruler of the Netherlands Duke of Burgundy. To avoid that concentration of power which had upset the balance in Europe, the electoral German princes had denied King Philip the imperial title, electing instead the late emperor's brother, Ferdinand I. Thus until the year 1700 both the Austrian and the Spanish branches of the House of Hapsburg awarded the Order. The Spanish Hapsburg line came to an end in this latter year on the death of Charles II, and after the ensuing 'war of the Spanish Succession' in which England under the brilliant generalship of the first Duke of Marlborough played a conspicuous and triumphant part, the crown of Spain was confirmed to another Philip, fifth of his name and a grandson of Louis XIV of France. Whether or not on the accession of a Bourbon dynasty of princes in Spain the sovereignty of the Golden Fleece should have reverted to the Austrian Hapsburgs, it is a fact that kings of Spain continued to make awards of the decoration right down to the abdication of Alfonso XIII, in 1930.

In England, scriptural and classical associations apart, the economic importance of the wool trade in the later Middle Ages may well have contributed to the popularity of the lamb as an emblem of blazonry, though, like so much else in the world of those days, religious associations were never far away. One need only refer to the custom of impaling the Lamb with the Cross of St George. Many English inns still flourish under the sign of the 'Lamb and Flag', suggesting strongly that these ancient establishments were either built on former monastic property, or were originally founded by hotel keepers who had begun their careers as stewards and butlers of ecclesiastical houses before the Dissolution.

In heraldry the three commonest forms of blazon of this animal are the Paschal Lamb (Fig 105), the Fleece (as for the Toisson D'Or) (Fig 106) and the Ram's Head caboshed (Fig 107).

The Dog This domestic animal has always been popular in heraldry, largely because the part it played in the chase was highly regarded in feudal society. The modern breed of fox hound was unknown in the Middle Ages, and the three breeds of dog usually emblazoned were the Irish wolfhound, the grey-hound, and the talbot.

The wolfhound with its long shaggy coat was the most popular for hunting purposes, but curiously has figured infrequently in blazonry.

The greyhound, then employed for the chase, unlike the modern creature of the racing track, has figured more frequently in Scottish arms than in English (Fig 108).

The talbot, a slender, smooth-haired animal with large spaniel-like ears, was very popular in England. In English heraldry any dog other than a wolfhound or greyhound was always referred to as a 'talbot'. It figures, not unnaturally, on the arms of the great family that bear its name and became Earls of Shrewsbury. The first earl as Sir John Talbot founded his family's fortunes on his ability as a general in the first part of the fifteenth century. Although Bernard Shaw in *Saint Joan* makes his Earl of Warwick refer to him disparagingly as 'a mere fighting animal', this view does not seem to have been shared by his contemporaries who valued both his courage and his military skill. In the reign of Elizabeth I the sixth Earl of Shrewsbury, a Privy Councillor, was the custodian or gaoler of Mary Stuart between 1569 and 1585, a position he did not relish and which only his loyalty to the English Queen kept him for resigning. Indeed to preserve any sort of relations with a prisoner anointed Queen whom many considered to have a better title to the English throne than Elizabeth herself, and who was the centre of every Catholic plot, would have taxed the patience of a saint. No doubt George Talbot, the sixth Earl, was strengthened in his resolution by his wife, the formidable Bess of Hardwick. (Fig 109)

Other animals popular in medieval heraldry were the horse, the ox and the hind (emblazoned like a hart without antlers). As might be expected, the sixteenth- and seventeenth-century era of colonisation enlarged the scope of heraldic emblazoners by bringing to their notice a number of beasts previously little known or not known at all. Among such which have become popular with the emblazoner are the antelope, often found as a supporter, the elephant, the leopard and the zebra.

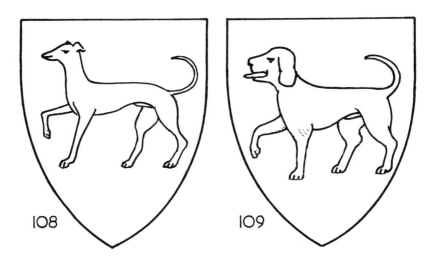

108   109

BIRDS

Almost as great a variety of birds as of animals has found its way into the heralds' repertoire, and we may describe a few of the more popular.

The Eagle This king of birds owes it pre-eminence not only to its size and majestic bearing, but also to certain legendary and historical associations. The eagle was the emblem the Roman legions displayed on their standards, and also became the symbol in art of the fourth Evangelist. In the Middle Ages the Holy Roman Emperors emblazoned the eagle with two heads, a practice followed by German princes dependent feudally on the imperial house who were permitted to include this charge in their armorial bearings. The Hapsburg archdukes of Austria who 'inherited' the elective monarchy continued to display the double-headed eagle on their arms down to the destruction of the empire in 1918, when there also disappeared the imperial German eagle of the Hohenzollern emperors who as Kings of Prussia had inherited this mark of blazon from the Margraves of Brandenburg. The Russian Tsars (Caesars) who also displayed this king of birds seem to have adopted it heraldically as a symbol of Russia's claim to have inherited the mantle of the Roman Empire of the East which had finally disappeared with the capture of its ancient capital of Constantinople by the Turks in 1453. In England the eagle figures much less frequently in early arms. Its first official appearance seems to have been on the arms of Richard, Earl (later Duke) of Cornwall, younger brother of King Henry III (1216-1272). But the occasion was when that prince was elected 'King of the Romans', a title bestowed by the electoral princes of Germany on the heir to the medieval emperor. As a charge on arms the eagle is not common in medieval heraldry, but both in that age and in later times the bird was popular as a crest. Heraldically it has usually been emblazoned with open wings ('displayed'), and more rarely with closed wings ('close'). (Fig 110)

The Falcon Falconry remained a popular aristocratic sport until the eighteenth century, by which time fox-hunting had taken the place of the more traditional forms of the chase. The sporting use of these birds of prey had at one time been restricted by law and ancient custom to certain classes of society, even the various breeds of hawk being carefully graded. Thus the peregrine, the finest of all, was regarded as a royal bird reserved for kings and royal princes. Noblemen employed merlins and goshawks, the male merlins being known as 'gerfalcon', while female brids were known as 'tiercelet'. The females were the larger birds. These, like the peregrine, were all long-winged birds trained to fly in open country and kill their prey by stooping (swooping) from a great height with lightning speed. In wooded country the goshawk and sparrowhawk, which were short-winged birds, hunted down game birds by sheer speed, following every turn of the quarry. It is, therefore, not suprising that great expense and care were lavished on the training and upkeep of these birds. The establishment of a royal falconry, for example, bore comparison with that of a race-horse training stable today. And so it is understandable that the falcon should be so popular a subject of blazon, especially in medieval arms. Some charges show not only the bird itself, but items of its harness such as the hood (removed only when a game bird is sighted), or the bells and jesses (strips of

light leather to which bells are fastened tied on the bird's legs to make it easier
to follow the swift flight). Sometimes we find emblazoned as a separate charge
the 'lure', which was a bunch of coloured feathers on a stock waved after the
kill to entice the falcon back to the gauntlet of its owner. Falcons were kept and
trained in 'mews' (a name derived from the traditional call of the bird), and
carried to the scene of the chase by the falconer, chained to a square wooden
frame on which they perched called a 'cadge'. (Fig 111)

The Swan This beautiful bird in the Middle Ages was often the principal dish
at the main course of banquets given by kings and great lords. In those
ceremony-loving days the roasted swan was carried in procession to the high
table on a silver charger, but with all its gleaming white plumage temporarily
restored. It was illegal to trap or kill a swan in England except on orders of the
king, and it is interesting to note that the bird is still protected from poachers
and destroyers of wild life by the game laws. Perhaps most swans in Britain
today are privately owned, but those found on the river Thames belong either
to Her Majesty the Queen, or to one of the two great livery companies of the
City of London - The Vintners' and The Dyers' Companies. Every year in the

month of July officials called 'Swan Uppers' wearing special livery patrol the river above Teddington Lock in launches and even rowing boats flying the royal banner or that of the appropriate livery company in order to determine the ownership of the new cygnets. Those belonging to the Queen are left unmarked, but those of the livery companies have their beaks nicked with special marks. In heraldry the swan is nearly always emblazoned with a ducal coronet and gold chain round its neck and is then called a 'Cygnet Royal'. The bird has very often been the subject of a crest. (Fig 112)

The Heron One of the few birds charged on very early arms. Herons' feathers were sometimes worn in bonnets as a decoration. A tuft of black herons' feathers is still combined with a plume of ostrich feathers to form the hat decoration for the Order of the Garter. This majestic bird was well known on the rivers and undrained marshes of Saxon and Norman England. It feeds on fish for which it has a voracious appetite, and lives in colonies, some of which remain in existence for centuries (Fig 113)

The Raven (Corbeau) This bird is another ancient charge. In literature and in legend the raven has usually been described as a bird of ill omen - one's mind inevitably turns to Shakespeare and to Poe - but the bird does have happier associations. For centuries there have been ravens at the Tower of London, and most people are aware of the legend that some great disaster will befall England when they forsake that fortress. Perhaps the legend should not be treated too lightly because in 1941 when England had her back to the wall Sir Winston Churchill as Prime Minister gave orders that the Tower ravens should be given special rations.

The Swallow (Hirondelle) This bird, the forerunner of summer in England, heraldically is not to be distinguished from the house martin, and is the 'temple-haunting martlet' of Shakespeare who could appreciate as well as any Englishman the glad meaning of the swallow's first appearance, flitting to and from the eaves of stone castle and thatched cottage roof. Tradition assigned five swallows or hirondelles to the arms of St Edward the Confessor, though of course official arms were not being granted at that date. Nevertheless, the principal charge on the arms of Westminster Abbey remains 'Azure, a cross patonce or between 5 hirondelles also or'. The medieval lords of Arundel at the end of the twelfth century adopted this bird as a charge, and today the Lords Arundel of Wardour bear arms 'Sable, 6 hirondelles argent 3, 2, 1'. (Fig 114)

Some birds have figured in blazonry more often as crests. Such are the peacock, the pelican, the ostrich, the cock and the dove.

The Pelican The many examples of this bird to be found in the history of heraldry, either as crest or emblazoned on a shield, bear witness to its popularity. Perhaps one reason is that according to medieval legend, the pelican was supposed to peck its own breast to draw blood to feed its young whenever food and water failed, and therefore presented to the emblazoners a fitting symbol of the spirit of self-sacrifice. It is not suggested, however, that there is any heraldic significance in the presence of the famous royal pelicans in

St James's Park. A favourite form of blazon was to depict the pelican pecking its breast with drops of blood issuing therefrom, and this is known technically as 'vulning itself'. (Fig 115)

Dove. This gentle creature has since very ancient times been regarded as the symbol of peace and love. The dove that Noah sent forth from the ark, the legend of Aphrodite being drawn in her chariot by a team of doves, the stories are legion. In heraldry the bird is emblazoned often with an olive branch in its beak and may be found as a crest (see note on *The Olive* later in this chapter).

FISH

Fish have not played so important a part in heraldry as have beasts and birds. However, we may note three which provided favourite dishes for an age dominated by the Church which demanded that no meat be eaten on Fridays and on all the week days of Lent.

The Pike (Luce) A freshwater fish, the pike or luce is usually emblazoned in pale, or on a bend or a bend sinister. It is included as a charge on the arms of the Lucy family, and such arms are known as 'canting' arms.

The Herring This fish was eaten in vast quantities in medieval Europe, and the North Sea herring fisheries brought great wealth to the North German coastal towns known as the Hanse ports, and at one time the English ports such as Great Yarmouth and Lowestoft. In the absence of modern refrigeration, the fresh fish were usually salted down and packed in barrels for distribution all over inland counties. It was only the rich and privileged who could own their own stew ponds and river fishing rights.

The Dolphin This 'fish' (a mammal, in fact, but believed in the Middle Ages to be a fish) is associated with classical legend, and therefore comes quite naturally to figure in the list of common heraldic charges. It may be charged in a number of positions, but the more usual is 'swimming' which is termed *naiant*.

114   115

Two molluscs must be added since they were popular as heraldic charges, though the shells only are emblazoned.

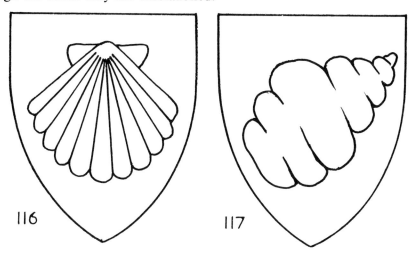

The Scallop This was a popular charge on medieval shields, probably because the shell was the emblem of the shrine of the apostle St James whose body was supposed to rest in the cathedral of Campostella in north-west Spain. This shrine remained a popular centre of pilgrimage throughout the Middle Ages, and men and women from England made the long and arduous voyage in the tiny ships of the time to win the right to wear the coveted shell badge of a pilgrim (Fig 116). The taunt of the Protestant reformers of Queen Mary Tudor's day has been immortalised in the nursery rhyme:

> Mary, Mary,
> Quite contrary,
> How does your garden grow?
> With silver bells,
> And Cockle shells,
> And pretty maids all in a row.

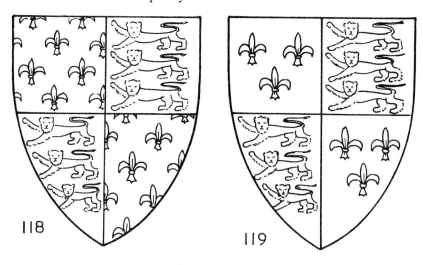

Queen Mary, who attempted to restore England to full communion with the Pope and the Roman Catholic faith was, of course, in the opinion of her Protestant adversaires, 'quite contrary' to the demands of 'pure religion'. The 'silver bells' of the rhyme refer to the little bells rung in churches at the moment of consecration in the mass; while the 'pretty maids' refers to the Queen's maids of honour who were noted for their beauty.

The Whelk No such religious significance can be attached to this mollusc, but its selection as a suitable object for heraldic charge bears witness to a popularity going back centuries before the rise to fame of the plebeian whelk stall of more modern times. The whelk is seldom emblazoned singly. (Fig 117)

FLOWERS AND OTHER PLANTS

Many of these have their heraldic origins in legend, while others have been chosen for emblazonment because of some symbolic association.

The Lily (Fleur de Lys or Lis) There are many species of this lovely flower, but it seems likely that the *Lilium candidum,* known in England as the madonna lily, which comes from southern Europe, is the species originally emblazoned by the heralds. Its pure white petals make a fitting symbol of purity, and so it was portrayed by many pre-Renaissance Italian artists who in their paintings of the Annunciation loved to portray the archangel presenting the Blessed Virgin with this white flower of purity. In heraldry the lily is for ever associated with the royal house of France. Legend has it that an angel brought down from heaven a golden lily to be henceforth the national emblem, but there is some doubt as to the identity of the king to whom this signal mark of favour was given. One legend says it was King Clovis who in the year 496 was baptised by St Remi, thus beginning the Christian history of France, while another ascribes the origin to Hugh Capet, who in 987 began the long line of Kings of France of the Middle Ages. In early blazon the royal arms of France are shown 'Azure, semée (powdered) of fleur de lis or', the azure fields representing the blue of heaven. Thus these arms figure also on the English royal escutcheon after King Edward III, by laying claim to the French crown in 1337, began the Hundred Years War. Over forty years later the French King Charles V (1366-1380) reduced the number of lilies to three of larger size; but it was not until the warrior English king Henry V revived the English claims and renewed the war in 1415 that the royal arms of England underwent a like modification. Kings of England continued to emblazon at least one quarter of their shields with the arms of France until at last in 1801, on the renewal of the Revolutionary wars against Napoleon, King George III relinquished the title 'King of France' which many of his predecessors had borne. This quartering was, in fact, reintroduced into the Royal arms of the sovereign in right of Canada by a proclamation of 1921. It is worth noting that to avoid confusion the heralds distinguish between the earlier form and the later one of three lilies referring to them, respectively, as arms of 'France Ancient' and 'France Modern'. (Figs 118, 119)

The Rose This flower is the emblem of England. It is emblazoned showing thorns (described as 'barbed'), and stamen (described as 'seeded'). Sometimes the flower alone is emblazoned; but when it is shown attached to stem and leaves it is described as 'slipped and leaved'. As a national badge this beautiful flower may owe its adoption to the white rose of York which was worn by the retainers of Richard, Duke of York, in the fifteenth-century wars against the house of Lancaster for possession of the throne. When those wars finally came to an end with the victory of Henry Tudor over Richard III at Bosworth in August 1485, the new king married the Princess Elizabeth, a surviving child of the late King Edward IV, and it is from about this time that the heralds began to emblazon a double rose or one in two tinctures to symbolise the union by marriage of the houses of York and Lancaster. It is significant that the title 'Wars of the Roses', was unknown in the fifteenth century, being a Tudor invention. The Tudor rose was embossed on the state liveries of the Yeomen of the Guard, and later on those of the Tower Warders, where it is still to be seen today. On the royal achievement the flower is emblazoned not as a charge but, with the thistle, the shamrock and the leek, on the green mound at the base known heraldically as the compartment. Of course the rose is not exclusively the badge of England, and many persons in the history of heraldry have chosen this flower as a charge on their arms, either singly or otherwise. Often it is emblazoned in its natural colours ('proper') but sometimes in a metal or tincture not natural to a rose. (Fig 120)

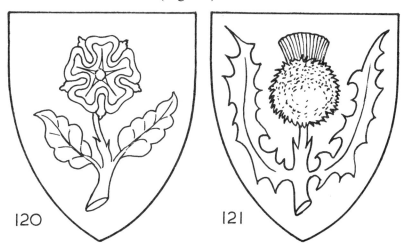

The Thistle Emblazoned together with its stalk and leaves ('slipped and leaved'), this flower is the emblem of Scotland. According to tradition, Kenneth Macalpine, who by uniting Picts and Scots in the middle of the ninth century became King of Alba, as the early Scottish kingdom was called, was once saved from a Norwegian ambush by an enemy soldier letting out a yell when he unwittingly trod on the sharp prickles of the plant. Although the lion rampant became the principal charge of the Scottish royal arms, the thistle at an early date was accepted as a national emblem, and remains today the central motif of the badge of the Most Ancient and Noble Order of the Thistle, that order of chivalry founded by King James VII and II in 1685 and refounded by Queen Anne in 1702 which ranks second only to the Garter. The thistle, like the rose and the shamrock, finds a place in the royal achievement, and like them is embroidered on the imperial pall or robe which the sovereign wears only at coronation. More down to earth, the thistle in the course of the last hundred years has become the distinguishing badge of Scottish teams for many international sporting events, as have the rose for England and the shamrock for Ireland. (Fig 121)

The Shamrock There can be few who do not know that this three-foiled green leaf is the floral emblem of Ireland, or that legend tells us that this 'three in one' leaf was used by St Patrick to explain the doctrine of the Trinity to the pagan Irish chiefs in the fifth century. Sprigs of green shamrock are still distributed to Her Majesty's Irish Guards every year on 17 March, St Parick's Day.

The Leek This is the senior emblem of Wales, but although there are several legends, the exact circumstances of the plant's becoming the Welsh floral emblem remain unknown. Shakespeare included an amusing piece of comedy in *Henry V* when the Welsh captain Fluellin forces Pistol to eat a leek. Some Welshmen continue to wear the leek as a button-hole on St David's Day (1 March).

The Daffodil This flower is often represented as an alternative floral emblem of Wales, and is worn on St David's Day by many Welshmen, being considered, no doubt, more suitable for a button-hole than a leek. There is no evidence to explain how this flower came to be associated with Wales, though the fact that the day of the patron falls just when the wild daffodil, sometimes called the Lent lily, is beginning to flower, may have suggested the adoption of this beautiful plant.

The Palm Because of its associations with the entry of Christ into Jerusalem at the beginning of the week that heralded his crucifixion and rising from the dead, the palm has always stood for both Christian martyrdom and victory. Since the ninth century the Church has celebrated the Sunday before Easter by preceding high mass by a procession of clergy bearing palm branches and singing hymns. In this they were following a still more ancient custom dating from the fourth century when the Roman Empire for the first time officially recognised the Christian religion. The first pilgrims to Jerusalem reported on their return that it was the custom on Palm Sunday for the Bishop of Jerusalem to ride on an ass supported by his clergy carrying palms over the actual route taken by Jesus and his disciples. In the Middle Ages all those who were fortunate enough to make the long and difficult pilgrimage to the scene of Christ's Passion were as a badge of distinction allowed to wear a small silver palm branch, and were henceforth known as 'palmers'. It also became customary for painters, illuminators and sculptors to depict the holy martyrs holding palm branches in their hands to distinguish them from those saints who had not been called on to shed their blood for Christ. In heraldry the palm has figured as a shield charge and as the embellishment of a crest.

The Olive Pre-eminently the emblem of peace, the 'olive branch' was never popular with warrior kings and princes; so it is perhaps natural that this plant should rarely be found on the achievements of knights, whose main occupation was fighting. It does, however, figure on a number of shields and crests of corporations and ecclesiastical bodies. It is, of course, the oil obtained from the olive that forms the base of the holy oils used by the Church in its sacraments. The plant is usually emblazoned as a branch 'slipped, fructed and leaved' in the beak of a dove, or as a branch held in the hand. The scriptural significance of both olive and dove would readily be appreciated in past ages. Occasionally, the whole olive tree is charged 'eradicated' (uprooted). The olive was a charge on the arms of the ancient Tallow Chandlers' Guild.

The Laurel In ancient Greece this tree was associated with the worship of the god Dionysus. Thus, at the original Olympic Games held in the god's honour it became the custom to crown the victors with laurel wreaths. A later age saw this symbol of victory crowning the heads of Roman generals driving in procession through the streets of Rome on their day of 'Triumph' granted by the Senate. The great Julius seems to have extended the fashion to all formal occasions, though whether this was intended to be a constant reminder to the Romans of his perpetual dictatorship, or, as some believed, because being a vain man he wished to hide his premature baldness, it is impossible to discover. The example being set, it was but a small step for the laurel wreath, now formalised in gold leaf, to become the diadem of the Caesars. The Middle Ages saw the imperial laurels pass to the Holy Roman Emperors of Germany, and finally in official sculpture and pictorial representation to the monarchs of post-Reformation western Europe. In England the coins of Charles II and the early Hanoverian kings show the monarch's head crowned with the laurel wreath. So also was the head of Elizabeth II sculpted in the early coinage of her reign. In heraldry the laurel in wreath form figures as a chaplet on some shields, and as a sprig or branch on some crests.

The Oak Especially in England has the oak tree been respected as an emblem of strength, perhaps because it had long been the dominating tree in those great forests that covered so much of Saxon and Norman England. From the days of King Alfred to those of Nelson it was the oak that furnished most of the strong wood needed to build the ships of the English navy. In another context it will be remembered that Walter Scott made the Saxon knight, Ivanhoe, bear on his shield as his device an uprooted oak tree to signify the fate he shared with so many Saxons after the Norman Conquest.

Perhaps the two most famous oak trees in English history were Herne's Oak in Windsor Park and the Boscobel Oak near Worcester. The former was a gigantic old oak which used to stand not far from Windsor Castle. According to legend this tree was the meeting place for the demon hunter, Herne, who, accompanied by his fierce pack of hounds and ghostly huntsmen, could be seen on certain nights noiselessly chasing their quarry through the old Windsor forest. It will be remembered that Shakespeare ends *The Merry Wives of Windsor* with a scene of Falstaff and his jolly company dancing round this famous oak. The Boscobel oak sheltered the young King Charles II from the searching Roundhead soldiers on his flight in 1651 from the battle field of Worcester. While the soldiers searched beneath, the King, concealed by the leafy branches, lay all day in the arms of the royalist Colonel Careless. After the Restoration the gallant colonel changed his name to Carlos, and was granted arms: 'Or, on a mount in base vert an oak tree proper fructed or, surmounted by a fess gules charged with three royal crowns proper'. After the Restoration the anniversary of the King's entry into London, 29 May, being his birthday, was always celebrated in England as Oak Apple Day, and the author well remembers as a small boy at a Somerset prep school with his fellows picking sprigs of fresh green oak leaves to wear in the buttonhole every year when King Charles's day came round. (Fig 122)

The Apple This is perhaps the most common of a number of fruits that have found their way on to the escutcheons of armigerous persons. The choice of fruit has often been dictated by historical association, but sometimes by association with the family name, eg 'Applegarth', whose arms are 'Argent, three apples gules'.

The Garb This is the name heralds give to the sheaf of wheat, and it is a charge that became very popular. The standard work on British heraldry by A.C. Fox-Davies states that the earliest appearance of the garb in English heraldry is on the seal of Ranulph, Earl of Chester, who died in 1232. This powerful nobleman, whose father had been Justiciar to the crusading Richard I, had served King John to the best of his ability and became one of the principal regents, on John's death, for the boy-king Henry III. Ranulph's loyalty to the Crown, and his respect for the law and in particular Magna Carta, made his influence over English political life of his period of great importance. He was perhaps the richest and most powerful of all the barons of the first half of the thirteenth century, and also became Earl of Lincoln. It seems likely that the ancestors of the Grosvenor family whose head today is the Duke of Westminster inherited their name from a still more distant ancestor who attained power and wealth by inheritance from the old earls of Chester. The 'gros' means 'fat', and the second part of the family name may have come from the old French 'venour', which meant 'a hunter'. The arms of the Grosvenor family are 'Azure, a garb or'. It may be of interest to record that Queen Victoria's creation of the dukedom of Westminster for the head of this family was the last occasion in the history of the peerage on which a non-royal duke has been created. (Fig 123)

The Broom This flowering bush with the little yellow blooms is the famous *planta genesta* or *plante genet* which gave its name to the longest-reigning dynasty of English monarchs. It is said that the name Plantagenet is derived from the sprig of this *plante genet* which Count Geoffrey of Anjou, the second husband of the Norman Empress, Matilda, herself the only surviving heir of King Henry I, wore as a good-luck charm on his helmet. He was of course the father of the first Plantagenet king, Henry II.

Other fruits commonly depicted as charges and items of crests are pears, pomegranates, figs, oranges, strawberries. The strawberry leaf became the principal motif of the ducal coronet (see Chapter 7).

CELESTIAL OBJECTS

There are many examples, ancient and modern, of arms charged with celestial devices. Sun, moon and stars naturally suggest themselves as fitting objects for heraldic display because of their symbolic significance, as well as their natural beauty.

The Sun The sun is nearly always emblazoned with rays streaming from the disc. This is described by heralds as 'the sun in splendour'. The rays are alternately straight and wavy, a piece of symbolism suggesting the light and heat derived from this heavenly body. In some examples the human face is depicted on the solar disc. (Fig 124)

The Moon Usually emblazoned in crescent form, the moon occasionally appears in heraldry as a disc, but without rays. It is then to be described as 'in plenitude'. In crescent form it may be emblazoned in a number of positions. With horns pointing up to chief it must be described as 'crescent', horns pointing dexter as 'increscent', and horns pointing sinister as 'decrescent'. (Fig 125)

The Star (Estoile) This celestial object is to be distinguished heraldically from the molet, which it resembles, by having six *wavy* rays issuing from it, and by never having its centre pierced. The estoile, as it is usually called, is found on the shield charged both singly and in numbers. It also finds a position as an item of crests. (Fig 126)

Other celestial objects used include Thunderbolts, Clouds and Rainbows. (See for example, the escutcheons of the BBC and the Metropolitan Water Board.)

OTHER INANIMATE OBJECTS

The number and variety of devices used by heralds that do not fall into one or other of the categories already described is so great that any attempt to classify them must be doomed to failure. We shall attempt only to describe a few common objects that are emblazoned in stylised form and are, therefore, not so obviously recognisable, and a few that have interesting historical origins or connections. The reader will, nevertheless, bear in mind that in principle there is practically no limit to the number of different objects that may be used as charges, crests or even supporters in modern times, ranging from shuttles in saltire for a Lancashire cotton town to engine wheels for British Railways.

Crowns and coronets, falling naturally into a special category and often denoting rank as well as being depicted as common charges, will be described in a separate section. The same may be said of bishops' mitres, croziers, etc, which are dealt with in the short chapter on ecclesiastical heraldry.

126   127

128   129

The Clarion This is simply a musical instrument emblazoned in a stylised form. (Fig 127)

The Fetterlock A shackle and padlock. This charge was borne as a personal badge successively by the Plantagenet dukes of York and King Edward IV. (Fig 128)

The Fountain In heraldry this is usually emblazoned in stylised form as a roundel with horizontal wavy bands alternately argent and azure. (Fig 129)

The Galley (ancient) Emblazoned with three masts, the sails furled or in full sail. The galley may or may not be shown with the oars in action. (See also Lymphad, below.) (Fig 130)

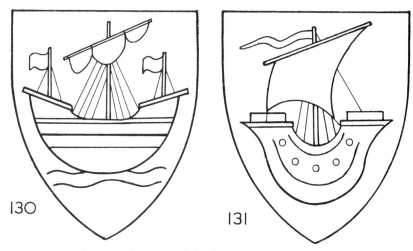

The Guttee A display of drops of liquid, usually associated with some major charge, eg 'pelican in its piety', or vulning itself (see under Birds above), and a cloud with rain drops. The term is 'guttee de sang' (blood), 'd'eau' (water), etc.

The Lymphad The same as an ancient galley, but with one mast only. (Fig 131)

The Pheon A stylised arrow head. The chief characteristic is the engrailed inner edge - engrailed is the term used to describe a partition line that is indented or serrated. When emblazoned without the engrailing they are often referred to as 'broad arrows'. (Fig 132)

The Seaxe This was the original Saxon battle-axe, and a very formidable weapon indeed. By the eleventh century the seaxe had lost its distinctive notch to become the double-headed battle-axe fixed to a holding staff 3½ft long that King Harold's Huscarls wielded with such terrible effect against the Norwegians at Stamford Bridge. These same troops, the finest in Europe, nearly won the day at Hastings against the Norman cavalry, and the respect Duke William's knights had for this weapon is borne witness to by the near-contemporary illustrations in the Bayeux Tapestry. (Fig 133)

The Castle Figures 134 and 135 show the conventional blazon of the castle, though many variations are possible. When either *castle* or *tower* - the former is commonly represented by a gatehouse flanked by round embattled towers, the latter by a single embattled tower or turret - is crowned with several little turrets, this charge is to be described as triple-towered. The embrasures at the summit of the towers and on the parapet wall between are referred to as 'crenelles', and the pieces of wall rising between as 'merlons'. A castle wall thus emblazoned must be described as 'crenellated' or 'embattled'.

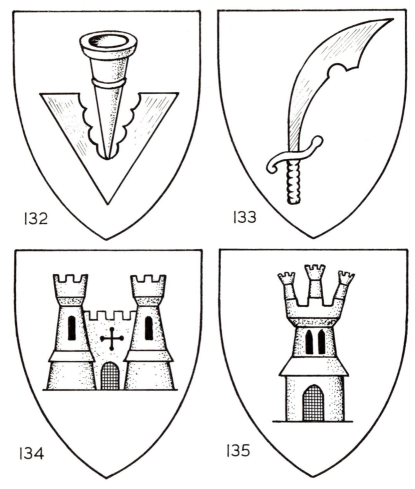

In Europe the great age of the military fortification known as the castle was between the mid-eleventh century and the late thirteenth, though such fortification had existed for centuries before and continued to play some part in military history until at least the mid-seventeenth century. In the earlier period when the 'dark ages' were ending, the feudal lord all over western Europe was building to shelter his peasantry from robber barons those fortifications which in many cases were to become the small towns of the Middle Ages.

Castle building took a great step forward with the arrival on the European scene of that nation of military geniuses, the Normans. They were of course to learn much about the art of military engineering from their contacts with Greeks and Turks during the Crusades; but in England the circumstances of the Conquest of 1066 for a time imposed severe limitations on the fashion of these constructions. Faced with the prospect of permanently holding down a conquered race numbering perhaps two million - William the Conqueror's army at Hastings had not exceeded 7,000 - the Normans employed Saxon slave labour to raise earthen mounds of 80-100ft high at one end of flattened courtyards which they surrounded by deep ditches and high banks of earth crowned with wooden palisades. Entrance to such a castle was by a simple wooden drawbridge over the ditch leading to a heavily defended wooden gatehouse. Within the courtyard, or 'bailey' as it was called, were set up lean-to sheds for horses and cattle, a blacksmith's forge, a communal hall and a chapel.

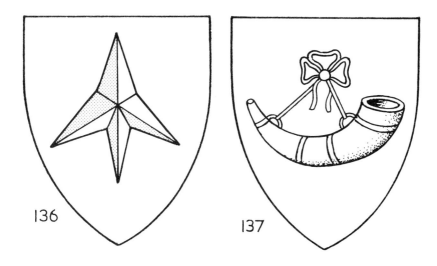

A wooden ladder led to the top of the mound, called the 'motte', which was flattened to receive a wooden tower itself surrounded by a palisade. Here lived the castellan or lord of the garrison, and from this height sentries surveyed the countryside for possible attack. With the aid of such fortifications William I was able to consolidate his conquest. The only stone castles he built himself were the White Tower of London and the Keep of Colchester. In the more settled conditions later in the century the bailey palisade was replaced by a stone 'curtain wall', while on the motte, where it was firm enough to stand the weight, was raised a round crenellated fortification known as a 'shell keep' (those at Restormel in Cornwall and Arundel in Sussex still exist).

By the mid-twelfth century the motte had disappeared, and in its place had been erected the big stone keep with corner turrets, rising in the middle of the old bailey to a height of some 90 ft. This was on four floors. The ground floor was used for stores of food, weapons and ammunition. Entrance was by a flight of stone steps outside to a narrow door, and again steps down to ground level inside. This was to make it more difficult for enemy attackers. A spiral staircase in one of the corner turrets connected each of the floors, again a measure of defence. The first floor was the garrison room, the second the great hall where the lord and his officers dined and held their councils, while the top floor contained the private quarters of the lord and his family. Recesses in the walls contained bedrooms and a private chapel, while on the roof sentries kept a strict look-out. An important feature of the stone keep was the well which could supply a besieged garrison indefinitely with water. In normal times the soldiery lived in wooden buildings set up in the bailey as before. The next stage of development was the construction of towers or turrets jutting out at intervals along the curtain wall that surrounded the keep. The object was to allow archers defending the castle from attack to direct an enfilading fire on those attempting to scale the walls. The final development of this type of castle was to construct a strong gatehouse with a mechanically raised drawbridge, a portcullis, and concealed slits in the parapet immediately above the entrance to pour hot ashes or other unpleasant substances down on those attempting to storm the castle. It was found that rounded turrets resisted the stones hurled by such siege engines as the mangonel and trebuchet better than had the sharp edges of the old square constructed turrets. Excellently preserved examples of the stone keep may be seen at Rochester, Guildford and Newcastle.

The final development of the age of castle building came with the great fortifications raised in Wales by King Edward I at enormous expense, an entirely different type of castle that was practically impregnable and capable of maintaining a very large garrison for a year on end without relief. The stone keep was no longer needed, and in its place was a double line of walls, an outer and a higher inner, strong gatehouses and a strong stone barbican at the entrance to the drawbridge leading to the first gatehouse. Inside there were inner and outer courtyards now known as wards, and many more stone buildings for housing the garrison and ministering to the needs of defence. There were variations, but the type as built at Beaumaris is known as the concentric castle on account of its double surrounding wall. Thereafter the importance of castle building began to grow less, one of the last in the old style being Bodiam in Sussex which was constructed in 1385 to defend that part of the coast from attack by the French.

Today most of the ancient castles of England are in ruins, but the Tower of London, Dover Castle and Carnarvon, still royal fortresses, have not been allowed to suffer the fate of so many of the others. It used to be said that the invention of gunpowder and the cannon inflicted the death blow on ancient castles; but though increasing efficiency of the new weapons made these stone fortresses no longer impregnable, they were still useful in times of war or insurrection, as witness the part many a castle played in the Wars of the Roses, or even two hundred years later in the Civil War.

The Caltrap Originally named the 'cheval trap', this was a sinister instrument of ancient origin used against cavalry in war. It was an iron frame with four points, and when placed on the ground in any position always had one point facing upward to wound the foot or leg of the horse stepping on it. (See 'Canting Arms' - Trappes, p81) (Fig 136)

The Bugle-Horn In heraldry this is charged as a curved horn, sometimes with strings or ribbons attached. With ribbons it is described as 'stringed', and the tincture is added if different from that of the horn. In the same manner when the bands round the horn bear a different tincture, it is described as 'veruled' or 'viroled' of that colour. The appropriateness of such a charge to the arms of, for example, the Forrester family (Argent, a bugle-horn sable viroled or, stringed gules) will be obvious. Originally constructed out of the horn of cattle, the instrument served as a recognition signal for foresters and other persons in the days when large tracts of forest were still reserved for the royal and noble hunt. Children will call the mind the famous horn of Robin Hood. (Fig 137)

The Maunch (Manche) This charge represents the sleeve and pendent lappet of the outer garment worn by ladies in the twelfth century. It seems likely that this article of clothing found its way into heraldry because it became a common 'favour' that ladies bestowed on their favourite knights to wear in battle or tournament. It is a matter for speculation whether the lady actually cut off the lappet from the garment she was wearing at the time, or came provided with the favour cut from some other garment. We are on more certain grounds when we state that the more likely object of knightly devotion, the handker-chief, did not make its appearance until the reign of Richard II whose fastidious nature led him to order the Court tailor to produce little squares of silk material for his courtiers who were in the habit of wiping their noses on their sleeves when they were suffering from colds in the head. (Fig 138)

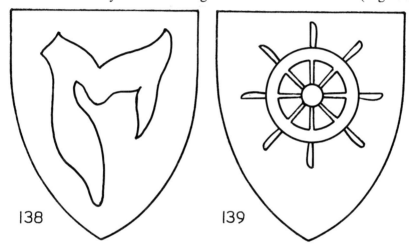

138   139

The Wheel Many forms of this common object have found their way into heraldic blazon, including in modern times the railway wheel (arms of British Railways, and of Swindon). In more ancient times it was the Catherine Wheel that was emblazoned. This wheel is named after the fourth-century saint of that name, who, according to legend, was tortured on that instrument before suffering martyrdom because she resisted the advances of the pagan Roman Emperor Maximius. We are told that this redoubtable Christian lady also routed in argument the combined efforts of the college of learned pagans at Alexandria where she suffered. Her body was discovered by the monks of the monastery on Mount Sinai in the fifteenth century. The monks seem to have claimed that the saint's body was translated from Alexandria by angels. Both the Roman Church and the Church of England honour her day in the calendar on 25 November. This saint must not be confused with St Catherine of Siena, the principal patron of Italy, who died in Rome in the year 1380 after a life of extraordinary sanctity and mortification of the flesh. (Fig 139)

The Key It is usual for two or more keys to be charged. When in saltire the wards should point upwards and outwards. Keys are more usually found in ecclesiastical blazonry, being the emblem of St Peter the Apostle who was given by Christ the power 'to bind and to loose'. In England the arms of the archbishopric of York are, 'Gules, two keys in saltire argent, in chief a royal crown or'. The crown may signify that the ecclesiastical province of York was once part of the ancient Saxon kingdom of Northumbria. (Fig 140)

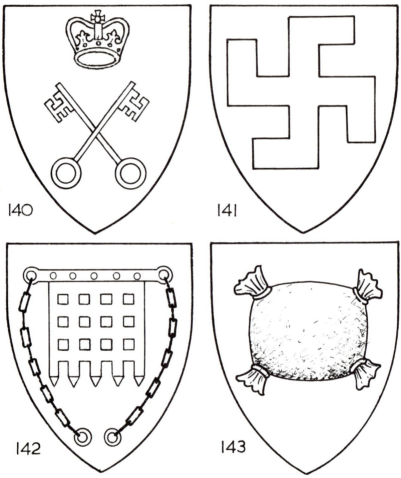

The Fylfot Fox-Davies informs us that this curious charge is better known by its 'early name', *Swastika*. Its origin is unknown, though some authorities believe that in the East it was used as a symbol of good fortune. If such was indeed the case, the swastika's associations with the West, at any rate since 1933, have been singularly unfortunate. The word 'Fylfot', was adopted, it would appear, because long before the symbol came to have political associations it was used to 'fill the foot' of windows. (Fig 141)

The Portcullis This charge is more usually found as a badge, and will be described later. The blazoned figure is of course based on that stout grating which was lowered by a winch from a position immediately above the castle entrance to provide an additional defensive barrier. One or two still exist in working order, such as the portcullis at the Tower of London. (Fig 142)

The Woolpack In medieval arms the woolpack makes a frequent appearance both as a shield charge and as an item of a crest. By the fifteenth century wool and woollen cloth had become England's principal export and source of economic wealth. The sheep bred in England and Wales produced a particularly fine-quality wool which was in demand for cloth-making all over Europe. The best wool came from the Yorkshire dales and the Cotswold Hills. In the north the Cistercian monks of Fountains and Riveaulx abbeys were the greatest breeders; but all over England the wool merchants would set out in the season to buy up the crop from the farmers to take to the staple ports (fixed places through which the export of wool was compulsorily directed), for export to the continent. Many merchants grew rich from this trade, as the size and architectural magnificence of many still existing merchant houses bear witness. After the various processes of cleaning and carding had been completed the raw wool was packed in 'sarplers' and carried by pack horses - the commercial transport of the age - to the warehouses of the merchants to await export. By the reign of Edward IV (1461-1483) the tax collected on every 'pound' of wool exported, and on every 'tun' of wine imported from Bordeaux and the Rhine ports had become a major source of the royal revenue. Thereafter for over two hundred years it became customary for the Parliament summoned to recognise the accession of a new monarch to vote 'tonnage and poundage' for the life of the new king or queen, and it was a source of bitter recrimination and serious financial embarrassment to King Charles I in 1625 when that monarch's first Parliament, suspicious of his religious and political intentions, voted him this tax for one year only!

Though today the heavy steel industry and various forms of electrical engineering have long displaced the pre-eminence of wool in the economy of Britain, and countries like Australia, Russia and Argentina have long outstripped Britain in number of sheep and in actual wool production, it is an acknowledged fact that the town of Leeds in Yorkshire still produces the finest quality cloth and suitings for men in the world. Perhaps this economic fact will go some way to justify the retention below the throne in the House of Lords of the crimson-covered 'woolsack' which for over five hundred years has been the official seat of the Lord Chancellor presiding over the High Court of Parliament. (Fig 143)

The Flambeau Always emblazoned as an old-fashioned torch or firebrand and always depicted with flames. In days when wax candles were so expensive that their use was practically restricted to the royal palace and church altars, the torch or flambeau set in iron sconces fixed to castle or manor house wall provided the only source of light in the dark winter evenings. These torches could also be carried in the hand. They were usually made of resinous wood specially treated, though in blazon they frequently appear as moulded containers.

The Tilting-Spear To be distinguished from the lance and javelin which have slender, straight shafts, the tilting-spear has at the holding end a narrow grip followed by a wider and heavier end piece for balance. It is always emblazoned with the sharp point used only rarely in tournaments for combats *à outrance*. The most famous example from history of this ancient charge is found in the 'canting arms' of William Shakespeare, 'Or, on a bend sable, a tilting-spear of the field'. These arms were granted to the poet's father, John Shakespeare, by Sir William Dethick, Garter King of Arms, in 1596. Although John Shakespeare had been Bailiff of Stratford (equivalent to mayor), he had fallen on evil days financially, and was no longer chief citizen. It seems that in making the grant the Kings of Arms took into account the fact that, unlike John, Mary Shakespeare, the poet's mother, was of gentle blood. These arms were confirmed to the poet in 1606. (Fig 144)

144

145

146

147

CHAPTER 5

The Rules of Blazon

The rules which have come to be accepted by heralds have evolved over a period of many hundreds of years. They fall naturally into two groups: those governing position and description of charges on the shield; and those that have to do with the correct reading of a blazon.

POSITION AND DESCRIPTION

Rule 1.   One object is placed in the centre of the shield (Fig 145).
Two objects are placed either 'in pale' (Fig 146) or 'in fess' (Fig 147).
Three objects are placed either '2 and 1' (Fig 148) or 'in chief' (Fig 149) or 'in pale' (Fig 150) or 'in a bend' (Fig 151).
When there are more objects, the number and order must be declared, eg '3, 2, 1' (Fig 152).

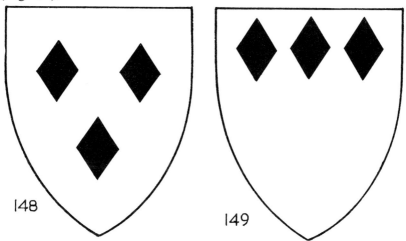

This is the rule for objects emblazoned on a shield not charged with ordinaries or sub-ordinaries. It will be seen in the next section that these ordinaries can themselves bear charges.

Rule 2.   When describing those parts of the human anatomy which are charged separately, the following rules will apply:
The Head:
i. state the racial characteristic, ie Saxon, Negro, Saracen or Savage.
ii whether affronté, or if in profile facing dexter or sinister.
iii whether couped or erased at neck or shoulders, or with face only shown ('caboshed').
iv. colour of hair (described as 'crined').
The Hand:
i. state whether dexter or sinister hand.
ii. whether open showing palm ('appaume'), or closed as a fist.

150

151

152

153

154

155

Arms and Legs:
i. these may be couped or erased at wrist, halfway between wrist and elbow, at elbow, at shoulder, or at knee or thigh.
ii. clothed in armour described as 'vambraced', in cloth as 'habited'.

These examples illustrated are savage's head (Fig 153), dexter hand appaume (Fig 154), cubit arm (Fig 155), arm couped at elbow (Fig 156), arm embowed (Fig 157), arm embowed and vambraced (Fig 158) and cubit arm habited (Fig 159). The arms of the Armstrong family (Fig 160) are described as 'Gules, three dexter arms vambraced and embowed argent, the hands closed proper'.

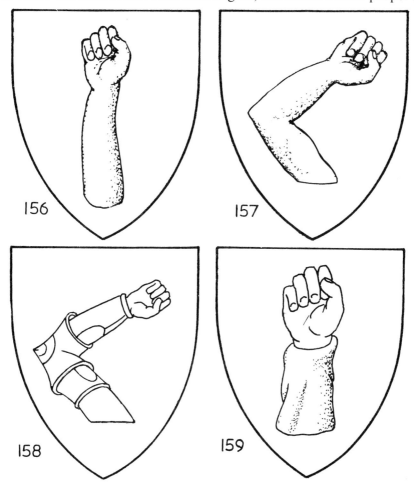

Rule 3.   Creatures, unless otherwise stated, are emblazoned in profile facing the dexter side of the shield. When they are shown facing the sinister side, the word 'counter' must be used, eg 'a lion counter passant'.

Rule 4.
i. Two animals emblazoned face to face are said to be 'confronted', or, alternatively, 'respecting each other'.
ii. Emblazoned back to back they are 'addorsed'.
iii. Emblazoned facing front, 'gardent' or 'affronté'.
iv. Looking back over the shoulder, 'regardant'.

Rule 5.   The positions and attitudes of certain creatures have been given their own special technical descriptions:

160   161

The Lion: Rampant (Fig 161), statant (Fig 162), passant (Fig 163), sejant
(Fig 164), couchant (Fig 165), coward (Fig 166), passant regardant (Fig 167)
and salient (Fig 168).

162   163

164   165

Animals of the Chase (deer, boar, etc): Courant (running) (Fig 169), trippant (walking) (Fig 170), lodged (sitting head erect) (Fig 171) and combatant (fighting) (Fig 172).

Birds: Volant (when flying) (Fig 173), rising (when rising) (Fig 174), displayed (both wings spread) (Fig 175) and close (wings close to body) (Fig 176).

178   179

When beak or legs or hooves are of a different tincture the description should read as 'Beaked and legged (gules)'.

Boutell distinguishes four varieties of 'Rising':

i. Wings elevated and displayed (spread each side of body with tips upward)

ii. Wings displayed and inverted (the same, but with wing tips facing down)

iii. Wings elevated and addorsed (spread back to back with tips upward)

iv. Wings addorsed and inverted (the same, but with tips downward)

Fish: Embowed (curved like a dolphin) (Fig 177), hauriant (in perpendicular position) (Fig 178) and naiant (swimming in horizontal position) (Fig 179).

Rule 6. When the claws, horns, tongue, etc of any animal bear a different tincture from the rest of the beast, they must be specified. These appendages must be referred to in the following terms:

Claws - 'Armed'   Tongue - 'Langued'
Horns - 'Corned'   Hair or Mane - 'Crined'

eg 'a lion rampant or, armed, langued and crined, hooves unguled, azure'.

Rule 7.   The head of human or beast on its own may be emblazoned in one of three ways:

'Couped' (cut off clean at the neck)

'Erased' (cut off at the neck with a ragged edge)

'Caboshed' (the face only emblazoned with no neck)

An animal or bird emblazoned with a coronet, chain etc round its neck is described as 'gorged', or 'ducally gorged', eg 'a cygnet (swan) royal ducally gorged' (Fig 180).

Rule 8.   The following terms are used to describe flowers and plants appearing as charges or crests:

'Flory'
'Semée'   } - Scattered with flower heads
'Powdered'

'Fructed' - Tree, bush or branch bearing fruit

'Barbed' - A rose emblazoned with thorns

'Seeded' - A flower showing seeds or stamen
'Leaved' - With the leaves emblazoned on the stem
'Slipped' - The blazon as if pulled or cut from branch or stem

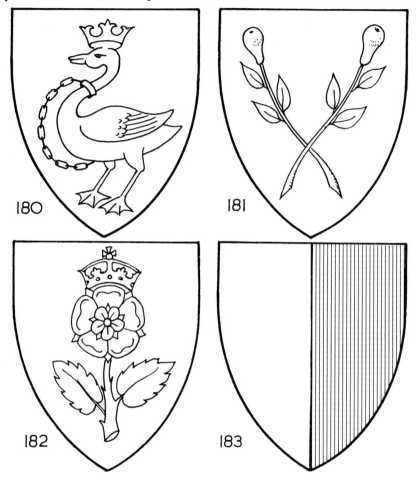

eg 'Two branches of pear saltirewise fructed and leaved proper' (Fig 181), or 'Red and white rose, barbed and seeded proper, slipped and leaved, and ensigned with royal crown proper' (Fig 182).

We may conclude this section with a short list of other terms commonly used by heralds:

'Attired' - a term used to describe the antlers of stag, hart or buck

'Cotised' - refers to the pattern formed by placing a bend, fess or chevron between two narrow bands

'Chausée' - displayed wearing shoes.

'Cloué' - an object studded or fastened with nails

'Crusilé' - a shield scattered with crosslets

'Dimidiation' - the practice of cutting in half two shields, and joining together the dexter half of the senior arms to the sinister arms of the junior arms. This method was so used at one time but not now when the shield is divided vertically down the centre. The total design of the arms of the husband is then displayed in the dexter half, and similarly for the wife in the sinister half. This is termed impaling as, for example, Brown (ie the arms of the husband) impaling Smith (ie the arms of the wife). It is true, however, that one finds in modern practise a relic of dimidiation for matrimonial purposes when the bordure of the husband's arms is, frequently, not carried down the central vertifical line of impalement.

    'Demi' - halved, that is the emblazoning of only half the figure of human or beast, eg 'a demi-man' or 'a demi wolf'

    'Double-queued' - with two tails, eg the wyvern

    'Fimbriated' - a narrow edging of a different tincture from the rest of the charge

    'Fourché' - description of anything that is forked

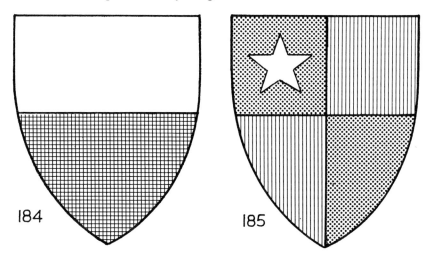

    'Gemel' - two or three annulets interlaced

    'Gobony' - a single row of checky squares

    'Humetty' - cut short at both ends (a cross humetty)

    'Infulae' - the ribbons hanging from the rear base of a bishop's mitre (see Chapter 9)

    'Issuant' - coming out of, eg 'a spear issuant from a dragon's mouth'

    'Laminated' - possessing scales

    'Lioncel' - a little lion

    'Martel' - a hammer

    'Nimbus' - a halo emblazoned round head of the Deity or saint

    'Nowed' - knotted, eg 'a lion rampant, double-queued nowed'

    'Pallet' - two or more pale-wise stripes

    'Pegasus' - a winged horse

    'Rouelle' - the rowel of a knight's spur (really a pierced molet)

    'Vulned' - an animal wounded and emblazoned with drops of blood

This list is not exhaustive, and in fact many heraldic terms and names not appearing have by implication been defined in other contexts in the book.

READING OF BLAZONS

We have now reached the stage where we can study the rules governing the correct reading of blazons. Contrary to popular opinion, these rules are simple and logical, the heralds having at all times taken the greatest care to make their meaning clear. Although the accidents of history have determined that much of the description of tinctures, charges and shield divisions should be in French, the language employed to describe a blazon is English.

Rule 1.   Describe first the colour of the shield background. This is known as the 'field', though in describing a blazon the word is never used. In a simple blazon the field will be all of one colour.

When the field has more than one tincture these will follow partition lines, and the word 'per' must be used, followed by the division line, and finally the tinctures, dexter and sinister or in chief or in base, in that order.

    i. per pale argent and gules (Fig 183)

    ii. per fess argent and sable (Fig 184)

    iii. quarterly gules and or, in first quarter a molet argent (for obvious reasons the word, 'quarterly' must replace 'per') (Fig 185). These are the arms of the De Vere Earls of Oxford.

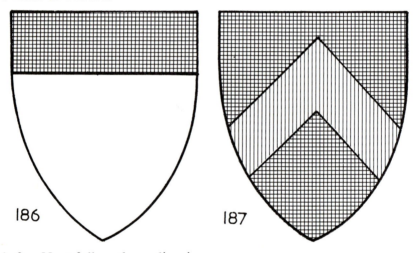

186   187

Rule 2.   Next follow the ordinaries:

    i. Argent, a chief sable (Fig 186)

    ii. Sable, a chevron gules (Fig 187)

Where there is more than one ordinary, mention first the principal ordinary forming the division:

    iii. Or, a fess sable between two chevrons gules (Fig 188)

    iv. Azure, a chief argent and a bend sable (Fig 189)

Rule 3.   Where an ordinary itself bears charges, these charges must be mentioned last in order to keep the proper order of description:

    i. Gules, on a chevron argent 3 crosses of Calvary sable (Fig 190)

    ii. Checky azure and argent, on a chief azure a sun in splendour between 2 ducal crowns or (Fig 191)

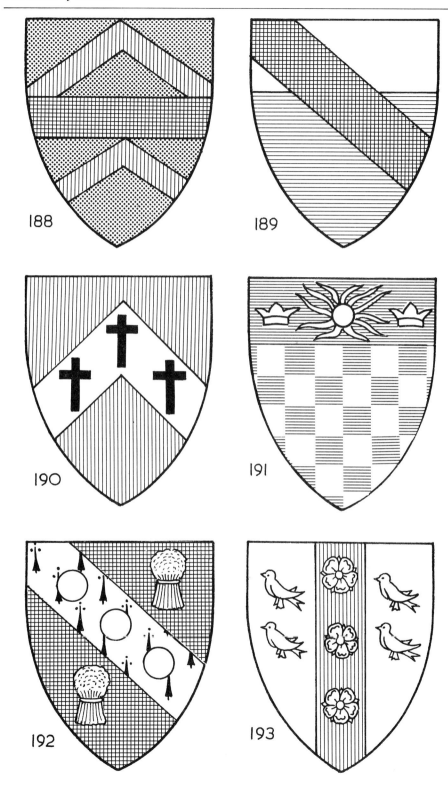

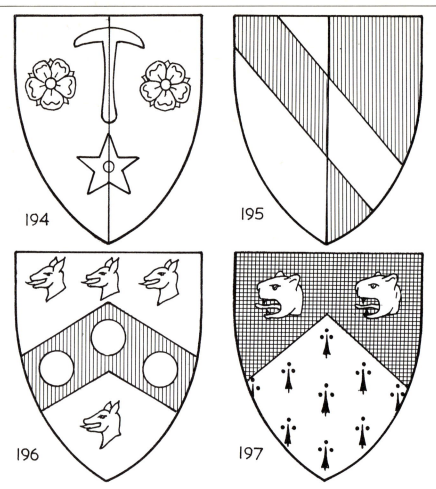

Rule 4   Where there are charges in the field as well as on the ordinary, the former must be mentioned first:

    i. Sable, on a bend ermine between 2 garbs or 3 torteau (Fig 192)

    ii. Argent, on a pale gules between 4 martlets also gules 3 roses barbed and seeded proper (Fig 193)

Rule 5.   Where there is a simple division of the shield by a partition line, both ordinaries and charges on either side or emblazoned across the partition line may bear the two tinctures of the field in reverse. Such ordinaries and charges are then said to be 'counter-changed':

    i. Per pale argent and gules, a pickaxe between 2 roses and in base a pierced molet, all counter-changed, the roses barbed and seeded proper (Fig 194) - Town of Audenshaw

    ii. Per pale argent and gules, a bend counter-changed (Fig 195) - Geoffrey Chaucer

The difference in description should be carefully noted between arms bearing an ordinary which itself is bearing charges, and an ordinary serving solely as a partition line:

i. Argent, on a chevron gules between 4 wolves' heads erased also gules 3 plates (Fig 196)

ii. Per chevron sable and ermine with 2 pards [leopards' heads caboshed] or in chief (Fig 197)

Rule 6   Two ordinaries, the pale and the fess, together produce the cross, which is itself an ordinary. The two complementary partition lines produce the simple quartered shield. This is sometimes called 'grand quarters' to distinguish this method of division from the more complicated one of emblazoning with many such divisions each called a 'quarter'. Further details on this emblazoning of many quarters must be left for consideration in the next chapter in the section devoted to the marshalling of arms. In the description of grand quarters, when each quarter bears a different charge the order must be from dexter to sinister beginning with the chief of the shield:

Quarterly 1 argent, a garb proper, 2 gules, a rose seeded and barbed proper, 3 azure, a chevron argent, 4 argent, a bend azure (Fig 198)

It sometimes happens that arms are repeated. A good example is that of the royal arms of England in 1415:

Quarterly 1 and 4 France Modern; 2 and 3 England (see Figs 118 and 119).

CANTING ARMS

We may end this chapter with some examples of what are known as 'canting arms'. This is the term used by the heralds to describe arms on which the charges have been chosen to suggest puns on their owners' names or professions. Although many of these are obvious, some are not so easy to recognise because words have changed their meaning or pronunciation in the course of centuries:

Shakespeare: Or, on a bend sable a broken spear of the 1st, the point steeled proper (see Fig 144)

Lucy: Gules, 3 luce (pike) in pale argent (Fig 199)

Shelley: Sable, a fess engrailed between 3 whelks or (Fig 200)

Applegarth: Argent, 3 apples gules (Fig 201)

Trappes: Argent, 3 caltraps sable (Fig 202). For a description and definition of a caltrap see page 64. The family name Trappes is thought to have been derived from the name of this medieval instrument.

198

199

200

201

202

203

CHAPTER 6

Differencing and Marshalling of Arms

DIFFERENCING OF ARMS

Anyone making even a superficial study of coat armour must be struck by the similarity of many arms. Often the only difference between one shield and another will lie in a small addition made to one of them. These marks of 'difference' are the herald's way of distinguishing between several members of one family, and of marking alliances between great houses. Remembering that in former days wealth and influence often depended on possession of property in land, we can easily appreciate the social and political importance of such unions. We may also appreciate that a society addicted to pomp and splendour took special pride in marking such changes in fortune in so public a manner as the heraldic art afforded. Certain laws passed in England from the reign of Edward I to restrict the alienation of property made it necessary in such a society also to distinguish between members of the same family who might hitherto have possessed an inherent right to emblazon those family arms. Known technically as 'differencing', certain marks of blazon were evolved over the centuries to give visual expression to this military and socio-economic requirement.

The Bordure This was an early form of difference. A good example is to be found in the official arms of Humphrey, Duke of Gloucester (d. 1447): 'Quarterly modern France and England within a brodure argent' (Fig 203). The fourth son of Henry IV, this Plantagenet duke shared the regency for the boy-king Henry VI with his elder brother, John, Duke of Bedford, when their eldest brother, King Henry V, the victor of Agincourt, died unexpectedly in 1422. In the event, the Duke of Bedford was compelled to spend most of his time as commander-in-chief of the English armies of occupation in northern France, ruling in the name of the boy who by the Treaty of Troyes had become also King of France. This left Duke Humphrey to manage affairs in England where he was not very successful, in part because he did not possess his elder brother's military or political ability, and in part because he was principally concerned to advance his own interests. After the death of Bedford and the disaster to English arms in France following French resurgence under Joan of Arc, a party arose in England led by the Cardinal Bishop of Winchester and the Duke of Somerset, leaders of the Beaufort line of Lancastrian descent from John of Gaunt, to oppose the weak policy of Gloucester who was eventually forced to surrender all political power.

Duke Humphrey is chiefly remembered for the bequest of his library books to Oxford University which still preserves them in the exquisite Gothic building named after him that is now part of the Bodleian Library. The Duke is also remembered for his building of the palace of Placentia on the banks of the Thames near the village of Greenwich. It was this palace that King Henry VIII was to enlarge and make the favourite residence of himself and his Tudor successors. More than a hundred years later the then decaying Tudor structure was pulled down, and on the orders of Charles II were raised the exquisite classical buildings that today are the home of the Royal Naval College, and were also, until recently, the home of the Royal Observatory and the Astronomer Royal whose office was established by King Charles. It is, therefore, right through Duke Humphrey's old palace that there runs the zero line of longitude for the whole world, the Greenwich Meridian. As a footnote, it is interesting to add that in the summer of 1971 Oxford University Archaeological Society by royal permission carried out an excavation of that part of the site of the old Plantagenet palace not covered by Wren's building, revealing for the first time for centuries the foundation lines of the various rooms, kitchens and other apartments of the old palace.

The Canton This mark of difference takes the form of a small square in the dexter chief of the shield, and bearing a charge signifying an augmentation to the original arms. The arms of the county of Wiltshire are 'Barry of eight argent and azure, on a canton a dragon gules', and the augmentation reminds us that Wiltshire was once part of the ancient Saxon kingdom of Wessex whose emblem was a red dragon. (Fig 204)

The Escutcheon of Pretence Emblazoned as a much smaller shield imposed on the centre of the original shield which bears the family arms, this 'inescutcheon' is often used to mark a marriage alliance by bearing the arms of the wife who is an heraldic heir: 'Quarterly argent and azure, on an inescutcheon of pretence gules a ducal crown or'. (Fig 205)

The Label Perhaps the most familiar form of differencing, the label is used to distinguish the arms of the eldest son from those of his father. In essence the label consists of a band or strip emblazoned across the chief of the family shield with three or more 'pieces' pendent from it. Any tincture may be used except silver which is reserved exclusively for members of the Royal Family. The arms of Edward, Prince of Wales, known to history as the Black Prince, are 'Quarterly France Ancient and England, a label argent' (Fig 206). The description is taken from the achievement displayed over his tomb in Canterbury Cathedral where he was solemnly interred in 1376, one year before the death of his father, King Edward III. If the Black Prince had lived to succeed his father, he would of course have displayed the royal arms without the label which would then have passed to his own son, Richard of Bordeaux, who in fact was destined to become King Richard II at the age of ten. The Black Prince's military achievements are too well-known to need relating here. We might, however, note that his handling of the crisis that resulted in the summoning of the 'Good Parliament' of 1376 which impeached Richard Lyons, the London Merchant, Alice Perrers, the King's mistress and Lord Latimer, the Chamberlain, all of whom had been proved guilty of embezzlement and grave crimes against the national economy, gave unmistakable signs that if he had lived to become king, the immediate fate of England might have been a much happier one.

There has for centuries been much speculation concerning the origin of the sobriquet of this eldest son of Edward III, 'Black Prince'. One theory is that he habitually wore black armour, though there is no contemporary evidence; another that he was subject, in spite of his renowned chivalric nature, to 'black' rages, as for example his morally indefensible order for the sacking of the town of Limousin and the massacre of its citizens solely on the grounds that they resisted English attempts to turn them from their allegiance to the King of France; and lastly, that in his final illness disease turned his skin black. In fact there is little evidence to show that he was given this name in his lifetime in England. One possible explanation is that the sobriquet originated with the French who, after the fashion of the time, claimed that his extraordinary victories at Crécy and Poitiers against vastly superior strength could only have been inspired by the Devil with whom this 'black' prince was in league!

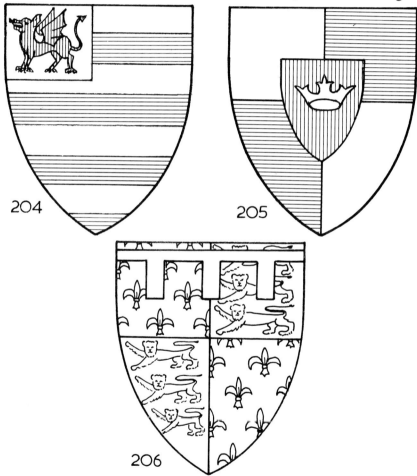

Cadet Differencing In the sixteenth century there came into general use the system of differencing the arms of younger sons by the addition of particular charges to the family arms:

     2nd son — a crescent (Fig 207)
     3rd son — a molet (Fig 208)

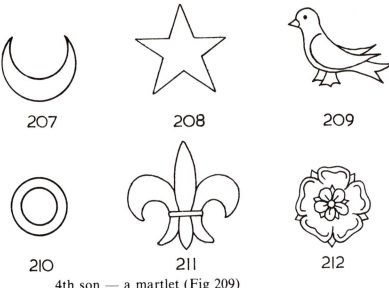

207   208   209

210   211   212

4th son — a martlet (Fig 209)
5th son — an annulet (Fig 210)
6th son — a fleur de lys (Fig 211)
7th son — a rose (barbed and seeded) (Fig 212)

These 'marks of cadency' were not always used because of complications resulting from additions to the shield, for example by marriage alliances.

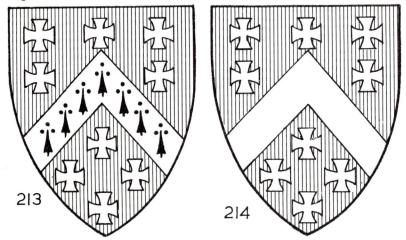

213   214

Difference by tincture and/or additional charge This was a method of differencing adopted not only by junior members of a family, but also by feudal dependents. Differenced arms granted to dependents of two famous families may be cited as good examples of this method. The Berkeley family arms are shown in Fig 213, the differenced arms in Fig 214; the Luttrell family arms are shown in Fig 215; the differenced arms in Fig 216.

Berkeley in the county of Gloucestershire had been a royal manor in Norman times. King Henry II (1154-1189) granted manor and castle to that family who took the name 'Berkeley'. It is a remarkable fact that Berkeley

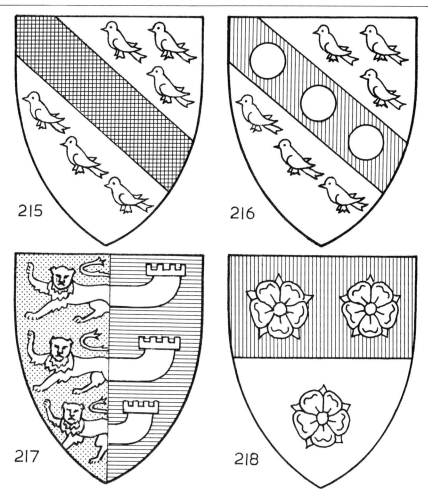

Castle has remained in the possession of this family as an actual residence to this very day, a period of more than eight hundred years. It was in Berkeley Castle that in 1327 by secret orders of the Queen's lover, the Earl of March, King Edward II was done to death in peculiarly revolting circumstances which was later to be made the subject of high tragedy by Christopher Marlowe.

The Luttrell family have owned and lived in Dunster Castle in west Somerset in the shadow of Exmoor since the fourteenth century. Although several members of the family in past centuries have performed signal service to the king, or distinguished themselves in other fields, no Luttrell has aspired to any greater honour than simple knighthood. It is on record that the head of the family in the early days of the nineteenth century declined the honour of a peerage, stating proudly that he preferred to remain an English gentleman with a name that had been borne with honour for five centuries! The famous Luttrell Psalter, once owned by the family but now a treasured possession of the British Museum, remains one of the principal sources of information for historians of fourteenth-century dress and agricultural custom by reason of its superbly executed illuminations.

MARSHALLING AND DESIGNING OF ARMS

MARSHALLING

Fox-Davies had defined marshalling as follows: 'The science of marshalling is the conjoining of two or more coats of arms upon one shield for the purpose of indicating sovereignty, dominion, alliance, descent, or pretension.'

Halving Arms (see also *Dimidiation* on p76). The arms of the town of Sandwich are: 'Per pale gules and azure, three lions passant guardant or dimidiating three ships' hulls argent' (Fig 217).

Sandwich was one of the seven (originally five) English Channel coast towns known as the Cinque Ports which in the twelfth century were given the responsibility of supplying and fitting out ships of war for the king's service for a period of forty days each year. If their service was required for a longer period, it was to be at the king's expense. In return, these ports were given certain privileges which included charters of liberty, the right to elect their own town government, and to elect certain leading citizens who came to be known as the 'Barons of the Cinque Ports' to represent them at coronations, where they wore special robes and carried in procession the canopy held over the king. This latter privilege they still have. The original constitution provided for a Lord Warden of the Cinque Ports to preside over the official activities of the barons. There is still a Lord Warden, although today his duties are purely ceremonial but the position is one of great prestige. He has at his disposal an official residence which is Walmer Castle, Deal. Past Lord Wardens have included the great Duke of Wellington who actually died while in residence at Walmer in 1851, the first Marquess of Reading, former Lord Chief Justice and Viceroy of India, and Sir Winston Churchill. The present Lord Warden is Sir Robert Menzies, KT, one-time Prime Minister of Australia. The other Cinque Ports are Dover, Hastings, Hythe and New Romney (with Sandwich, the original five), plus Rye and Winchelsea.

Parted per Fess As a partition line the fess can be employed to marshal two simple blazons: 'Per fess gules and argent, three roses barbed and seeded counter-changed.' (Fig 218)

Since early medieval times Southampton has enjoyed the reputation of being the main English Channel port, not excepting Plymouth. Modern dredging has helped much to make it possible for Southampton to maintain this reputation, so that the world's largest passenger liners can sail right up the estuary. Its pre-eminence as a port may be ascribed to several factors: it lies less than a hundred miles from London; and the geographical position of the Isle of Wight afforded a natural defensive protection from direct attack in the days of the French wars. To these may be added yet another powerful argument: the accident of the two channels, Spithead and Solent, to the open sea provides four high tides daily.

It is not possible to set down even a bare outline of Southampton's history. We may perhaps note that its proximity to King Alfred's capital of Winchester helped to promote its importance when that monarch was looking round for likely sites for the shipping yards that were to build the long ships of his new navy out of the oak from English forests. We remember that it was from Southampton that Henry V's invasion fleet set out to win the battle of Agincourt and conquer all northern France. In 1588 it was from Southampton that the English fleet of Howard and Drake was replenished when it ran out of powder and shot in its life-and-death struggle with the Great Armada. Finally, it was from Southampton that a large part of the allied invasion force set out for Normandy on D Day, 6 June 1944.

Per Chevron An interesting example of the use of the chevron as a partition line for marshalling is to be found in the arms of Sir John de Clarence: 'Per chevron gules and azure, in chief two lions rampant respecting each other and in base a fleur de lys, all or.' (Fig 219). Sir John de Clarence was a son of Thomas, Duke of Clarence, younger son of King Henry IV, who as Lord High Constable in the reign of his elder brother, Henry V, presided over the Court of Chivalry, and very possibly was responsible for the creation of the office of Clarenceux King of Arms.

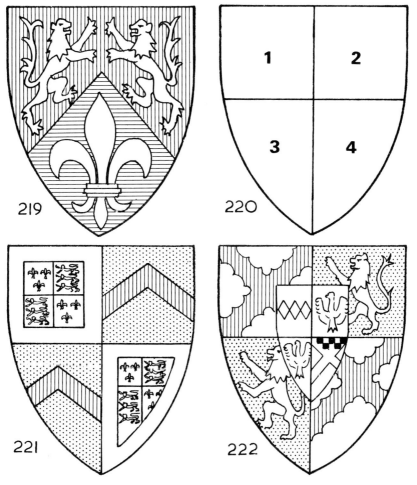

Quarter and Grand Quarters The shield is said to be quartered when it is divided by pale and fess partition lines. Each of the four quarters thus formed may bear a distinctive tincture together with ordinaries and charges; although in the simplest quartering the blazon on the first quarter is repeated on the last, while the blazon of the second is repeated on the third quarter. The correct numbering of quarters is shown in Fig 220. A good example is seen in the royal arms before the death of Elizabeth I in 1603 (see Fig 119).

Until the middle of the fifteenth century it was rare to divide and emblazon the shield with more than these four quarters. Thereafter, the increasing importance of the marriage of heiresses in an armigerous society created special problems. In some cases the inescutcheon was employed; in others what Fox-Davies calls the 'squeezed in' quartering, eg the King Maker's arms (Fig 1). This led to the system known as 'grand quartering' whereby the first and fourth quarters, and sometimes the second and third, are subdivided into four quarters.

An interesting example of simple grand quartering, if one may use the term, is found in the arms of Sir Edward Stafford, Duke of Buckingham: 'Quarterly 1 and 4, quarterly i and iv France Modern, ii and iii England, within the bordure argent of Thomas Woodstock; 2 and 3 or, a chevron gules [for Stafford]' (Fig 221).

Edward, Duke of Buckingham, premier peer of England and the last of his line, was executed on a bill of attainder for high treason in the year 1521. The Stafford dukes of Buckingham were directly descended from that Thomas, Duke of Gloucester, who was the youngest son of King Edward III. It was not a fortunate line. Thomas met his fate at Calais, supposedly murdered on the orders of his nephew, Richard II, while most of his descendants met sticky ends, including the last duke's father who had been beheaded at Salisbury in 1484 for his part in the first unsuccessful attempt to replace King Richard III by Henry Tudor. One of the articles of attainder against Duke Edward was that he had placed the royal arms in the first quarter of his escutcheon, thereby ostentatiously drawing attention to his royal descent. Although he was undoubtedly entitled to do so, this act coupled with the unwise public expression of scorn for the 'upstart' Tudor dynasty (so said his enemies who included the powerful Chancellor, Wolsey) was sufficient to bring down on his head the wrath of King Henry VIII who at that date, with only the Princess

Mary as lawful issue, was not unnaturally sensitive on the matter of the succession. Edward, Duke of Buckingham, was the last to hold the great office of Lord High Constable. One of his duties had been to preside over the Court of Chivalry and the royal heralds. Henceforth that duty was to devolve on the Constable's deputy, the Earl Marshal.

Inescutcheon in Marshalling '1 and 4 argent, a saltire raguly gules [Tiptoft]; 2 and 3 or, a lion rampant also gules [Powis]; for his wife, Cecily, on an inescutcheon 1 argent, three fusils in fess gules [Montague], 2 and 3 or, an eagle displayed vert [Monthermer], 4 gules, a saltire argent with a label gobony argent and sable [Neville]' (Fig 222). This is a fine example of the emblazoning of the arms of a wife on her husband's shield; also of the marshalling of those allied family escutcheons that in the Middle Ages signified concentrations of political power. Cecily, wife of John Tiptoft, was the daughter of Richard Neville, Earl of Salisbury. The fifteenth-century nobleman, John Tiptoft, Earl of Worcester, was the most flamboyant of all the early English renaissance nobility. He won a name for high scholarship, and earned the title of 'Butcher of England' for his severities to his political victims. Educated at Balliol College, he became Lord High Treasurer of England while he was still in his twenties. Towards the end of Henry VI's reign he made a pilgrimage to Jerusalem, and on his return stayed in Italy to study law at Padua where he disputed with the greatest scholars of the day. While in Italy he made a remarkable collection of Greek and Latin manuscripts which he afterwards presented to Oxford, his old university. He returned to England with the accession of the Yorkist King Edward IV, and after serving that monarch as Constable of the Tower of London, was appointed to the great office of Lord High Constable of England. It was in this capacity that he earned his savage nickname on account of the ruthlessness with which he did his best to exterminate the Lancastrians who had lost the throne in 1461. At the same time John Tiptoft remained a great patron of the arts and learning, and himself found the time to translate Cicero's *Essay on Friendship* and other classical works which Caxton was soon to print for the first time. When the King-Maker led the Lancastrians once more to victory in 1470 and Edward IV was once more forced to go into exile, Tiptoft was arrested by his enemies and arraigned for high treason. Found guilty and sentenced to death, he suffered on Tower Hill on 18 October 1470 with great dignity in the midst of a large crowd of citizens howling for his blood. This extraordinary man demonstrated his remarkable eccentricity in an eccentric age to the very last, beseeching the headsman to sever his head from his trunk in three strokes in honour of the Holy Trinity.

Augmentations of Honour A good example of heraldic augmentation is provided by a comparison between the original arms of the Churchill family and those borne in modern times. The old arms were: 'Sable, a lion rampant argent, on a canton argent a cross of St George' (Fig 223). The canton was added to the original arms of the seventeenth-century Sir Winston Churchill in the reign of King Charles II. The augmentations conferred on his son, John, first Duke of Marlborough, make up the arms as borne today by the Marlborough family: 'Quarterly 1 and 4 sable, a lion rampant argent, on a canton a cross of St George [Churchill]; 2 and 3 quarterly argent and gules fretty or, over all on a bend sable three escallops argent [Spencer]; over all an escutcheon of St George surmounted by an escutcheon azure charged with three fleur de lys or [France]' (Fig 224).

The young John Churchill was brought to the notice of King Charles II, it is said, by the favour of the King's *maîtresse en titre,* Barbara, Countess of Castlemaine; and that monarch, always quick to recognise talent, started him off on his brilliant army career. In the next reign Colonel Churchill was appointed second-in-command of the royal army that put down the ill-fated rebellion of the Duke of Monmouth in the last battle to be fought on English soil, at Sedgemoor in 1685. The most serious blight on Churchill's character is that three years later he deserted James II at Salisbury in his hour of need, going over to the side of the usurping William of Orange. But in mitigation it must be remembered that many Englishmen were troubled in their conscience at the time over their allegiance to a Roman Catholic monarch who had shown unmistakably his wish to suspend the laws of England that had safeguarded the Reformation settlement. Another factor influencing Churchill was undoubtedly the close friendship of his wife, Sarah Jennings, with the King's Protestant daughter, Anne. In the new reign his military talents were speedily recognised by William III, himself a general of European reputation, and Churchill was not only given a command in the allied army opposing Louis XIV in the Netherlands, but raised to the peerage as Baron Churchill. A few years later he was created Earl of Marlborough and designated to succeed the King in the chief command when William, already a semi-invalid, should die. With the accession of Anne in 1702 he was created first Duke of Marlborough, while his duchess was appointed Mistress of the Robes and Keeper of the Privy Purse, a key position in the political system of the day. With the support of Lord Treasurer Godolphin, for the next eight years the Churchills practically ruled Queen and country. Marlborough himself winning an immortal reputation as one of the greatest military geniuses of all time by his victories over the armies of Louis XIV at Blenheim (1704), Ramillies (1706), and Oudenarde (1708). Thereafter the family fortunes declined, and by 1713, aided and abetted by Mrs Abigail Masham at Kensington Palace, a Tory ministry under Robert Harley and Henry St John had secured the dismissal of the Churchills from all their offices.

The two inescutcheons on the Churchill arms, the cross of St George surmounted by the blazon of France, constitute an augmentation of honour granted the first Duke to commemorate his great victories over the French in the War of the Spanish Succession. The Spencer arms quartered represent the alliance by marriage of his daughter with Charles Spencer, Third Earl of Sunderland, from whose issue, the first Duke having no surviving male heir, by royal warrant the dukedom was allowed to descend. It was from this line that Britain's wartime Prime Minister had descended. He was the elder son of Lord Randolph Churchill, himself the younger son of the seventh Duke of Marlborough.

Blazon of Sixteen Quarters We may conclude this section with an example of more complicated quartering. As has been pointed out, blazons of sixteen or more quarters are more common in continental heraldry than in English or Scottish heraldry. One reason for this has been that in most European kingdoms custom and law have dictated far less restriction on alienation of property than English law has allowed. A curious social effect, and one which the classless society of today may find difficult to understand, was that before 1914 in the European monarchies a family's social position was likely to be determined by the number of quarterings the head of the family could display. Entrée to the court of the Austrian Emperor Franz Josef (1848-1916) was generally refused to those who could not produce an achievement emblazoned with at least sixteen quarterings. As with all history, the student must put himself in the mental and philosophical atmosphere of the age to understand how intelligent people could readily accept this situation. A study of Victorian and Edwardian English social history will prove beyond doubt that even on these more liberal shores the vast majority of the middle and lower classes accepted the dogma that a man was born into that station in life that God intended, and that it was his duty to accept that fact. And before our more 'enlightened' age condemns such selfish snobbery out of hand, it would do well to reflect that in the very great majority of cases there was respect between master and servant, each recognising the value and importance of the other in the general scheme of things.

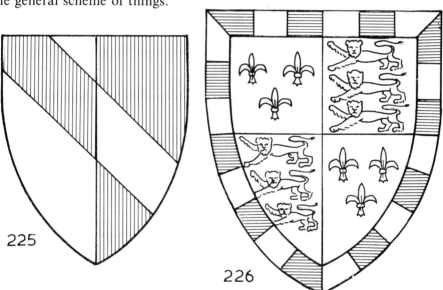

225

226

SOME METHODS OF DESIGNING ARMS

Counter-changing This is the term used for what Boutell describes as a 'reciprocal exchange of the tincture', when on a shield particoloured certain ordinaries or charges appear on both sides of the partition line bearing the tincture of the alternate side. Thus a shield parted per fess sable and or and charged with three roses would show the rose or roses on the sable side tinctured or, and those on the gold side tinctured sable. A simple example of counter-changing is found in the arms of Geoffrey Chaucer, 'Per pale argent and gules, a bend counter-changed'. (Fig 225).

Geoffrey Chaucer, the first great poet to write in the English language of his period, was probably born in 1340 - the exact date is unknown. He was the son of a London vintner, and in 1359 entered the service of Lionel, Duke of

Clarence. Later he served as a soldier in France in the army of King Edward III where he had the misfortune to be captured; but it seems that already his abilities were rated so highly in royal circles that the King himself paid for his ransom. Afterwards Chaucer entered the service of John of Gaunt, Duke of Lancaster, and his marriage to Philippa Roet, sister of Gaunt's third wife, Katherine Swynford, herself the mother of the Beaufort line of dukes of Somerset, no doubt helped to establish the poet in Gaunt's estimation. He was sent on various diplomatic expeditions abroad, and in 1372 visited the city of Florence where he met the historian Petrarch, and very likely Boccaccio whose great literary work, *The Decameron,* may have suggested the idea of *The Canterbury Tales.* Returning to England, Chaucer was appointed Controller of Customs for the Port of London, by a strange coincidence having his main office on a site where recently stood the headquarters of the Port of London Authority. In 1386 he was elected a knight of the shire for Kent in the Parliament of Richard II which met that year, and was also appointed Clerk of the King's Works for the royal residences and for Westminster Abbey. No doubt it was this rich and varied experience that enabled him to write so vividly and with such insight of people in all walks of life in the England of the late fourteenth century. *The Canterbury Tales* were written around 1387. Other principal works of Chaucer were *The Romaunt of the Rose* and *Troylis and Cryseyde* on whose pages, one of the first works to be printed by Caxton a hundred years later, Shakespeare most likely drew for his play based on the same Greek story. The Father of English Poetry died in the year 1400.

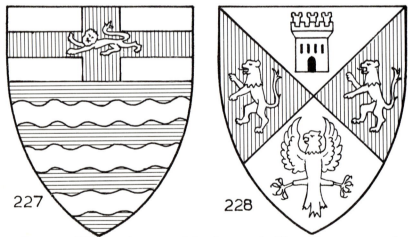

The Bordure The bordure, used in the marshalling of arms, was given the principal tincture of the field of the arms to be allied, and usually was itself charged with devices emblazoned on those arms. The Beaufort family arms are: 'Quarterly France Modern and England within a bordure gobony azure and argent' (Fig 226). This family, on whose head was conferred first the earldom, then the dukedom of Somerset, was descended from John of Gaunt, fourth son of King Edward III. Gaunt's eldest son by his first marriage, to Mary of Bohun, succeeded Richard II as King Henry IV (1399-1413). The Beauforts, descendants of Gaunt and Katherine Swynford, were legitimated by Acts of Parliament of Henry IV, but barred from the succession. They were allowed to bear the royal arms, but differenced with a bordure of the Beaufort livery colours of azure and argent. No doubt this was intended to provide visual evidence that this family, though of royal descent, was in fact barred from succession to the throne. The bordure disappeared with the accession by right of conquest of the Beaufort-Tudor prince who succeeded as Henry VII in 1485.

The Chief A very common method of marshalling simple blazons is to add charges to a chief. This is well illustrated in the arms of the old London County Council granted in 1914: 'Barry wavy of six azure and argent, on a chief of the last a cross of St George charged with a lion of England' (Fig 227). These arms were granted for the authority (now replaced by the Greater London Council) which was brought into being in 1889 to form the chief local government for the vast sprawl of metropolitan boroughs and suburbs beyond that had become modern London. Originally, the Romans had bridged the Thames somewhere near the site of London Bridge, and for 1,700 years there was only one London Bridge. The City itself was walled and separated by open fields from what are now continuous built-up areas, except for the road named the Strand linking the City with the royal palace and abbey of Westminster. The blazon of the City became the cross of St George with the sword of St Paul charged in the dexter chief. So, when the time came to devise new arms for Greater London, it was decided to marshal the arms of the City with a barry wavy base emblematic of the river Thames whose navigable waters provided the main reason for the advancement in wealth and importance of one of the greatest city ports in the world. The new Greater London Council's blazon is: 'Barry wavy argent and azure, on a chief gules a Saxon crown or'.

The Saltire Formed by a combination of the partition lines of bend and bend sinister, the saltire presents an alternative method of simple quartering to the cross. A good example is to be found in the arms of Disraeli: 'Per saltire gules and argent, in chief a castle triple-towered of the second, two lions rampant in fess sable, and in base an eagle displayed or' (Fig 228).

Benjamin Disraeli, Queen Victoria's favourite prime minister and leader of the Conservative party in Britain through the middle years of the reign, came of Jewish stock, though his father had embraced the Christian faith and had his famous son brought up as a Christian. Disraeli first made a name as a novelist, and though his novels are little read today, they must rank as literary works among the best writing of the century. His career as a statesman began comparatively late in his life, and it was not until the death of the Earl of Derby, the titular leader of his party in 1867, that he became the undisputed leader of the Conservatives. He was partly responsible for the policy of imperial expansion that was to dominate British political and commercial life in the last quarter of the nineteenth century, and it was during his last great ministry of 1874-80 that Queen Victoria was proclaimed 'Empress of India', a title to be borne by all her successors until King George VI relinquished it in 1947. On his retirement for the last time from the prime ministership Disraeli was created Earl of Beaconsfield and made a Knight of the Garter, then still a political honour. He died in 1884, his mantle descending to Robert Cecil, third Marquis of Salisbury, who was destined to become the last peer of the realm to hold the supreme office.

CHAPTER 7

Crests, Crowns and Coronets

CRESTS

The nature and purpose of crests has already been explained in Chapter 2. As long as armour continued to form the proper accoutrement of the fighting knight, crests had to conform to some sort of utilitarian design; but from the sixteenth century the armoured knight became a figure of the past, and his achievement was henceforth to be found only in heraldic blazon. One result was that much greater licence was allowed to the heraldic painters who, in particular, let themselves go in the designing of crests. The reader will be able to compare ancient and modern crests from the examples given below. A great deal can be learnt from a study of these appendages. Some commemorate events of national or local history, while others recall signal service to monarchs. In more recent times crests have been designed with the express purpose of symbolising a profession or trade, and this is especially true of achievements granted to boroughs, public corporations and colleges.

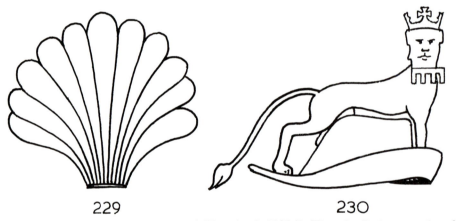

229   230

Humphrey de Bohun, Earl of Hereford (1301) The de Bohun earls of Hereford were powerful feudal lords in the thirteenth and fourteenth centuries. Earl Humphrey, who fought in Edward II's army against Robert Bruce at Bannockburn (1314), adopted a fan-shaped crest, probably made of boiled leather, as an additional protection against blows in battle (Fig 229).

Thomas Mowbray, Earl of Nottingham and Earl Marshal (1389) This was the Thomas Mowbray who a few years later was created first Duke of Norfolk of his line by Richard II. The official description of his crest is: 'On a chapeau, a lion statant guardant or, ducally crowned argent, queue extended, a label argent' (Fig 230).

Hatfield, Hertfordshire 'On a wreath of the colours an oak tree eradicated proper surmounted by a Tudor rose barbed and seeded' (Fig 231). The town of Hatfield was part of the royal manor of Hatfield where the young Princess Elizabeth was confined on the orders of her half sister, Queen Mary Tudor.

Legend has it that one sunny November day she was sitting beneath an oak tree in the park when Lord William Howard, Captain of the Queen's Guard, arrived to inform her that the Catholic Queen was dead, and that she was now Queen. Having gone for so many years in fear of her life, Elizabeth would not believe him until he gave her a ring from the late Queen's finger which, she knew, would never have left Mary while she was alive. The story continues that, convinced at last, Elizabeth quoted from Psalm 118 verse 23, the verse, 'This is the Lord's doing: and it is marvellous in our eyes'. If she did, it must have been an act of political expediency to impress the courtiers present, because the new queen with all her great qualities was never noted for her religious devotion. Hatfield House ceased to be a royal manor nearly fifty years later when King James I exchanged it with Robert Cecil for Theobalds, Lord Burghley's old house. Hatfield is still in the possession of the Cecil family, being the principal residence of the Marquess of Salisbury.

231   232

233   234

British European Airways 'On a wreath of the colours a sun in splendour superimposed by a swift volant sable' (Fig 232). This crest in heraldic language symbolised the efficiency of BEA with its 'swift' flights beneath the rising sun. (The arms consist of a fess between three astral crowns, the fess representing the sea separating Britain from the rest of Europe.)

United Kingdom Atomic Energy Authority 'On a wreath argent and sable, a sun in splendour or charged with a voided escutcheon gules, thereon a martlet sable' (Fig 233). In this modern crest power is symbolised by the sun, the ultimate source of all power, and by the martlet which figures in the arms of Lord Rutherford, the first man to split the atom.

British Antarctic Territory 'On a wreath of the colours a representation of the research ship *Discovery* with sails furled and flying the blue ensign at the mizzen peak'. The arms and crest of this new colony were originally granted to these British territories, then known as the Falkland Islands Dependencies, in 1952. The *Discovery* was of course the ship commanded by Captain Robert Falcon Scott, RN, on his expedition to the South Pole, which he reached some three weeks after Roald Amundsen discovered it in December 1911. As everyone knows, Scott and his brave companions perished tragically in a blizzard returning to base from their heroic journey.

Sir Francis Drake 'On a wreath of the colours a galleon under reef with banner of St George at mizzen, main and fore masthead, drawn round a terrestial globe with a cable by a sinister hand issuing from a cloud, all proper'. There is a story quoted by Fox-Davies to the effect that Drake was illegally making use of the arms of another family of the same name, who made complaint to Queen Elizabeth herself, whereupon the Queen said that she would grant Drake arms that would outdo those of his complaining namesake. Whatever truth lies behind the legend, it is a fact that Francis Drake was granted his arms, 'sable, a fess wavy between two estoiles argent', and the crest by Clarenceaux King of Arms (Fig 234).

CROWNS AND CORONETS OF RANK

The origin of the golden crown as an emblem of royalty is unknown. No doubt some form of official head dress was adopted by the priest-kings of quasi-legendary times, and surviving examples of bas-relief and sculpture show Egyptian, Babylonian, Assyrian and Persian monarchs all wearing on their heads distinctive and obviously symbolic decoration transcending the utilitarian helmet. There is, however, no indication that an actual crowning formed part of the elaborate initiation ceremonies of those early kings. By way of contrast, the Old Testament is full of references to golden crowns, and it seems likely enough that this royal emblem passed from the monarchs of the East to the kings of Jerusalem, even though an anointing with oil was the central act of king-making ('Zadok the priest and Nathan the prophet anointed Solomon king'). The Roman emperors of the West disdained this symbol of royalty, because Augustus had seen to it that the imperial authority rested not only on the supreme military command but also on absolute control of the old Republican magistracies which continued to function in the early empire. The diadem of the Caesars was the laurel wreath; but this symbol of republican days signified simply the Triumph accorded to victorious generals by the Roman Senate. It is almost certain that the golden crown passed to the monarchs of medieval Europe from the Byzantine emperors reigning from Constantinople. These Greek emperors were often in close touch with the oriental monarchies bordering their empire, and it is a fact that the Byzantine

Court became renowned for the formal magnificence of its ceremonial.

We cannot be certain when the golden crown made its first appearance as a royal emblem in England; but there can be little doubt that such a crown was worn by the Saxon King Edgar the Peaceable in the year 973 at his coronation by St Dunstan, the Archbishop of Canterbury. Moreover, it was Dunstan who devised the form of ceremony that has been used with little variation ever since for English coronation services, and he borrowed many of his ideas from Byzantium. Throughout the Middle Ages this coronation crown was regarded as a sacred object. It never left the coronation church, remaining in the charge of the abbots of Westminster who 'released' it together with other items of the regalia only for the solemn and rare occasion of a coronation. The crown with which medieval artists and sculptors portrayed Norman and Plantagenet monarchs was known as the 'Second Crown', put on first for the procession and progress from the Abbey after coronation. It is this crown that the Conqueror wore three times a year when he met his Great Council of barons in the earliest form of Parliament, and it is this and not the Crown of St Edward that English monarchs of a later day wore when they met their Parliaments and received foreign ambassadors.

The Imperial State Crown worn by Queen Elizabeth II when she opens a session of Parliament in state, though actually made for Queen Victoria at her coronation, is in fact the descendant of this medieval Second Crown. In form it may differ considerably in that the latter most probably lacked the imperial arches, and certainly was not so gorgeously jewelled.

Finally, we should note that it became the custom for warrior kings like Richard I, Edward III and Henry V to lead their armies wearing a battle crown fitted over the helmet. This diadem, was not, strictly speaking, a crown at all, but a circlet of gold worn with the sole purpose of enabling their knights and pike men to identify them in the all-enclosing and identical armour of the day.

> I saw Mark Antony offer him a crown - yet t'was not a crown
> neither, 'twas one of these coronets.

Casca's speech in *Julius Caesar* shows that in Shakespeare's day the difference between a crown and a coronet was well recognised. In fact this 'little crown' had made its first official appearance in England more than two centuries earlier when John of Gaunt, third son of King Edward III, was invested as Duke of Lancaster in 1361. At the ceremony of investiture the record tells us that in addition to investiture with the sword in its scabbard, which was placed by the monarch round the neck, a piece of ceremonial invented for the creation of earls dating from at least the eleventh century, the new duke was invested with a gold circlet for the head, and a gold rod or verge which was placed in his hand. The earls were not to receive the coronet until the middle of the sixteenth century, and the barons not until 1685. We may believe that the other degrees of peerage received the coronet between these dates. At the same time some attempt was made to distinguish between the different degrees, though it was not until the eighteenth century that the coronets of dukes, marquesses, earls, viscounts and barons, the five degrees of British peerage, received the distinctive forms they bear today (see below).

In modern times coronets of peers and peeresses are worn only for the rare occasion of a coronation, since the medieval ceremony of investiture has not taken place since the reign of James I and VI (1603-1625). At the ceremony of the introduction of a new peer to Parliament in the House of Lords he and his two sponsors wear the parliamentary robe of their degree (scarlet wool cloth, and ermine and gold bars to the number of their degree, with black cocked hats). The only surviving ceremony of investiture is that of a new Prince of Wales, and those who witnessed the Investiture of Prince Charles at Carnarvon in 1969 were in fact gazing on a piece of ceremonial that, with the exception of the nearly similar investiture for the Duke of Windsor in 1911, had not been seen for nearly three hundred years.

Crown of St Edward The present crown, worn only for the coronation, was made for the coronation of King Charles II in 1661, the original regalia having been destroyed by the orders of the Commonwealth government that preceded the Restoration. It is believed that in the original St Edward's Crown the four imperial arches were not depressed as they are today. (Fig 235)

Imperial State Crown More heavily jewelled than St Edward's, this crown is worn by the Queen when she opens Parliament in state. It is the modern replica of the medieval 'second crown' of monarchs. (Fig 236)

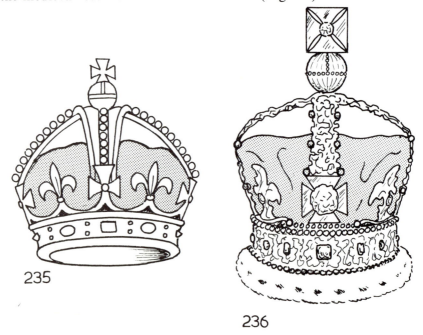

235

236

Coronet of Prince of Wales Fig 237 shows the diadem worn by the late Duke of Windsor when as Prince of Wales he was ceremonially created and installed at Carnarvon Castle in 1911. The present heir apparent, Prince Charles, at his installation in 1969 wore a specially designed 'trendy' coronet, presumably thought to be in keeping with the times. The common factor of both coronets was that they were given only two imperial arches as opposed to the sovereign's four.

Coronet of Duke Silver gilt with eight gold strawberry leaves on the rim (Fig 238).

Coronet of Marquess Silver gilt, four gold strawberry leaves and four silver balls atlernately, the latter a little raised on points above the rim (Fig 239).

237   238

239   240

24I   242

Coronet of Earl Silver gilt, eight silver balls raised on points, with gold strawberry leaves between the points (Fig 240).

Coronet of Viscount Silver gilt with sixteen silver balls resting on the rim (Fig 241).

Coronet of Baron Silver gilt with six silver balls at equal distances resting on the rim (Fig 242).

As distinct from continental custom, British crowns and coronets of peers are worn over crimson velvet caps of estate which appear as a kind of lining. The caps of peers have a short embroidered tassel at the top. The coronets of peeresses are similar in design, but smaller and deeper. In heraldic display of the achievement of a peer of the realm, the coronet of rank is emblazoned below the crest and resting on the shield, as distinct from the royal crown which is emblazoned below the crest but resting on the helmet.

HERALDIC CROWNS AND CORONETS

As distinct from the crown and coronet of rank, the heraldic crown may be emblazoned as a charge on a shield, as part of a crest, or on the head or round the neck of human, animal or bird charged as crest or supporter. A creature thus emblazoned with a golden coronet round its neck must be described as 'ducally gorged'. Saxon, ancient and celestial crowns are usually emblazoned gold or silver, while other types of crown may take any tincture.

Saxon Crown Figures sometimes as a charge on a shield, but more usually as a crest coronet. In heraldry this crown often symbolises Saxon associations, as in the case of the ancient borough of Bury St Edmunds - 'Azure, three Saxon crowns each pierced by two arrows, crossed in saltire, points downward, all or'. Crest: 'On a wreath of the colours a wolf sejant guarding between its paws the head of St Edmund crowned, all proper'. The reference is to the martyrdom by the Danes of Edmund, King of East Anglia, last of the kings of this ancient state which was one of the seven kingdoms of Saxon England (Fig 243).

243   244

245   246

Ancient Crown This is an elaboration of the heraldic ducal coronet. Paradoxically, its origin is very modern, as it was first granted in 1956 in the arms and badge of the Heraldry Society. (Fig 244)

Ducal Crown This heraldic crown or coronet is quite distinct from the ducal coronet of rank, and would be perhaps more suitably referred to as a 'crest coronet', to avoid confusion and because it is more often than not emblazoned in the crest. Technically, the ducal or crest coronet differs from the duke's coronet of rank in showing only three of the five strawberry leaves assigned to dukes. This type of heraldic crown is no longer granted by the Kings of Arms. (Fig 245)

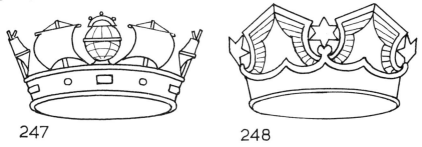

247 248

Mural Crown One of the commonest forms of heraldic crown, it is often charged on the shield in civic arms. The mural crown has frequently been granted as a crest to high-ranking army officers. Its distinctive features are the masoning and embattlement which are usually emblazoned proper. (Fig 246)

Naval Crown Emblazoned as a circlet from which rise alternate sterns and sails of ships, the naval crown was a very popular grant to the arms of distinguished naval officers in the eighteenth century when actions at sea were more common than they later became. Both Admiral Lord St Vincent and Admiral Collingwood (Nelson's second in command) embodied naval crowns in their achievements. (Fig 247)

Astral Crown This is a modern blazon composed of wings and stars set on a rim, and is used heraldically as the aviation counterpart of the naval crown. It figures as a crest coronet in the achievement of Marshal of the Royal Air Force Viscount Portal of Hungerford, KG, who was the Chief of Staff of the Royal Air Force through the greater part of World War II. (Fig 248)

Eastern Crown A plain rimmed circlet with five visible triangular plain spikes rising from the rim, the eastern crown is granted as a crest only to high-ranking persons in the imperial services who have served in India and the East. (Fig 249)

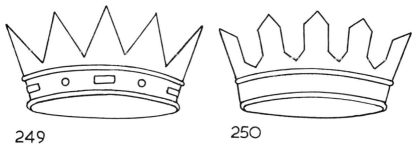

249 250

Crown Vallary This crown is in the form of a plain rim from which rise pieces in the shape of which the tincture, vair, is emblazoned. Five pieces are usually visible. (Fig 250)

Palisado Crown This heraldic crown was originally identical with the Vallary crown. It may be distinguished today by the fact that it is emblazoned with seven pieces resembling high palisades rising from the rim, in contrast to the five triangular pieces of the Vallary crown. (Fig 251)

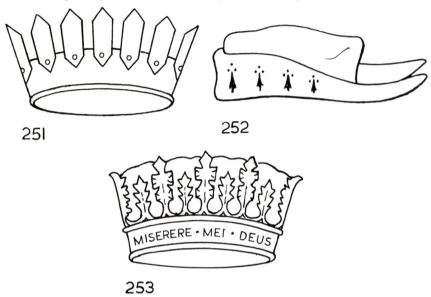

251   252

253

The Chapeau This is the 'Cap of Estate'. It seems that as regards its use in heraldry it has developed from two distinct sources: the cap of dignity which until the beginning of the eighteenth century was granted only to peers; and the hat which covered the top of the heraldic helmet until mantling was introduced. It has been noted that since the end of the seventeenth century this cap of dignity has actually been worn inside the coronet by peers of the realm. Originally its bestowal at the ceremony of creation by the sovereign had formed a separate part of that ceremony, and until the reign of Charles II the barons had to be content with the cap only, being denied the coronet. The *Cap of Maintenance* carried before the monarch at the State Opening of Parliament is in effect the royal form of the cap of dignity which was formerly worn by the king on certain state occasions when he did not wear his crown. It was Henry VII who set the precedent of combining the two, a fashion to be followed by the peers two hundred years later. In Fox-Davies's words 'Until the reign of Henry VIII the Royal crest, both in the case of the sovereign and all the other members of the Royal Family, is always represented upon a chapeau or cap of dignity'. The usual tincture and design in a crest is gules with a turned-up ermine lining, though other tinctures are not uncommon. Another practice is to rest the crest on a chapeau instead of on a wreath or torse. (Fig 252)

Crown of King of Arms This section may fittingly be concluded with illustration and brief note on the crown or coronet of kings of arms. In the fifteenth century there may have been a ceremony of 'coronation' for kings of arms on their creation; certainly there was a ceremony of baptism when water from a silver gilt cup was sprinkled over them. Today, alone among the heralds of the College of Arms, Garter, Clarenceux and Norroy, together with the

Lord Lyon King of Arms for Scotland, Bath King of Arms, the King of Arms of the Order of St Michael and St George and the King of Arms of the Order of the British Empire put on their crowns during a coronation at the moment the Archbishop places St Edward's Crown on the head of the monarch. It is at this supreme moment that the assembled peers also put on their coronets. These heralds' crowns formerly had engrailed rims. They are now plain, but have engraved round the rim the words of the 51st Psalm: 'Miserere mei Deus secundum magnam misericordiam tuam' (Have mercy upon me O Lord, according to thy great goodness). From the rim rise sixteen oak leaves, alternate leaves being higher than the others. The crowns of Garter, Clarenceux and Norroy are of silver gilt. (Fig 253)

CHAPTER 8

The Description of the Achievement and some Famous Arms

DESCRIPTION OF THE ACHIEVEMENT

We have now reached the stage when the whole achievement may be properly described in the heralds' language. Each item has been described in detail, and all that remains is to set forth the correct order in which the items should be mentioned, together with a few technical terms necessary to introduce them.

Shield This item comes first. The blazon should be described in accordance with the rules set down in the preceding chapters.

Wreath This item is nearly always tinctured in two colours, those of the field being the commonest. Livery colours may be used where these are avilable to the owner. Description must begin: 'On a wreath of the colours...' or 'On a wreath of argent and azure...' etc.

Crest This follows immediately on reference to the wreath, and follows the pattern set forth in Chapter 7.

Mantling The mantling or *lambrequin,* as it is sometimes called, will be in two tinctures, usually of the field. In Scotland the Lord Lyon has granted all peers a red mantling lined with ermine. In England the College of Arms grants mantling of various colours, but specifies that while colours form the outside, metals almost invariably form the lining. One other rule is that the mantling of the arms of the Sovereign and of Princes and Princesses of the Blood must be of gold, the Sovereign's lining of ermine, and that of other members of the Royal Family of argent.

Supporters Bearing in mind that the possession of supporters is a privilege granted to certain classes only, the reader should begin: 'On either side a griffin ...' (both supporters being identical), or 'Dexter a lion...Sinister a...' (where the two supporters differ).

Motto It is not really necessary to mention the motto at all, unless it is the subject of an actual charge on a shield (eg arms of Oxford University); but when it is placed at the base of the achievement it may properly be described last. When the motto forms part of, or is entwined with, the crest, it may more properly be mentioned at that point.

Helmet Although the heraldic helmet is undoubtedly one of the items of the achievement, it is unnecessary to describe it because the rank of the owner will be clearly indicated by design and position (Chapter 2).

Coronet of Rank For similar reasons this item of the achievement of a peer of the realm does not need to be mentioned.

SOME FAMOUS ARMS

ROYAL ARMS (IN SCOTLAND)

Quarterly 1 and 4 Scotland, 2 England, 3 Ireland, the whole encircled with the collar and pendent of the Most Ancient and Most Noble Order of the Thistle. On a royal crown proper a lion gules sejant affronte crowned and holding in the dexter paw a sword proper and in the sinister paw a sceptre or. Supporters, dexter a Scottish unicorn crowned, gorged with coronet comprising fleurs de lys and crosses pate crined, queued or and maintaining the banner of St Andrew, sinister a lion rampant guardant royally crowned for England maintaining the banner of St George, the whole on a mound [compartment] vert from which spring thistles and roses.

PEER OF THE REALM (DUKE OF ARGYLL)

Quarterly, 1 and 4 gyronny or and sable [for Campbell], 2 and 3 argent, a lymphad, sail furled with pennant at masthead and banners on both castles gules proper. In saltire behind the escutcheon, in bend dexter a baton gules, semee of thistles or, ensigned with an Imperial Crown proper, thereon the crest of Scotland [for Hereditary Great Master of Royal Household in Scotland], in bend sinister a sword proper, hilt and pommel or [for Hereditary Justice-General of Scotland]. On a wreath or and sable a boar's head or, langued gules and armed argent. Mantling gules lined double ermine. Supporters, on either side a lion rampant guardant gules, langued and armed azure. Mottos: VIX EA NOSTRA VOCO over crest, and in base NE OBLIVISCARIS. The achievement resting on a compartment vert.

The dukes of Argyll, who are hereditary chiefs of the clan Campell, have their principal seat at Inveraray Castle in Strathclyde. As Earls of Argyll they left their mark both on the history of Scotland and on that of Great Britain after the union of the two crowns in 1603. The earldom was created by King James III in 1467, and the first Earl at one time held the important office of Lord High Chancellor of Scotland. A hundred years later the fifth Earl led the army of Queen Mary Stuart against the rebels under her half brother, James Stuart, Earl of Moray, at Langside in 1567, but victory was snatched from the royalists at the last moment through the Earl, their leader, suffering an apoplectic fit at a critical moment during the battle. After Queen Mary had fled to England to become the prisoner of Queen Elizabeth, he made his peace with Moray, now Regent for the infant James VI, and later, after Moray's assassination, was appointed Chancellor by the new Regent, the Earl of Morton. The eighth Earl, Archibald Campbell, was in 1641 advanced to the dignity of a marquisate by King Charles I on the eve of the Civil War, but saw it as his duty to defend the Scottish Presbyterian religion against the attempts of the King to supplant it by introducing an episcopal church.

The first Marquess of Argyll led the almost united forces of Presbyterian Scotland to victory over the loyalist James Graham, Marquess of Montrose, whose defeat and capture were followed by his execution. After the execution of King Charles I, Argyll transferred his support to the young Charles II living in exile, and was a leading member of the committee of Scottish lords who, disappointed by the failure of the English Parliament to establish Presbyterianism in England, now invited the young King to Scotland as their monarch. It was Argyll himself who placed the crown on Charles's head at the coronation ceremony at Scone, the ancient crowning place of kings of Scotland. After the Restoration his loyalty became suspect and he was arrested and condemned to death. After his death Charles II had the Act of Attainder repealed, restoring to Argyll's son the estates and dignity of the earldom. In the reign of James II he supported the attempt of the Duke of Monmouth to depose the Catholic James VII and II, but, like the unfortunate eighth earl, was captured in his own native Argyllshire (now Strathclyde), and beheaded in Edinburgh. His son, the tenth Earl and third Marquess, was a staunch supporter of the Revolution which placed the Dutch William III on the throne. In 1701, he was created first Duke of Argyll. The ninth Duke in Queen Victoria's reign married Princess Louise.

A BARONET (ARMS OF SIR A. HOWARTH, BART)

'Azure on a bend between two stags' heads couped or as many garbs gules, in chief centre his badge as a baronet. On a wreath of the colours issuant from grass proper a stag's head gules, attired and gorged with a chain or. Mantling azure lined or.'

The dignity of baronets was created by King James VI and I as a means of raising money to support his Protestant plantations in Ulster. Later much the same device was attempted for colonial settlements on Nova Scotia. Sir Nicholas Bacon, Lord Keeper to Elizabeth I, and himself the father of a future Lord Chancellor, the essayist, Francis Bacon, was the first baronet. Baronets belong to an hereditary dignity, and have precedence above knights bachelor, but below Companionships of the Garter and Thistle and Knights Grand Cross of the other orders of chivalry. Baronets cannot sit in the House of Lords. Known as the 'Bloody Hand of Ulster', the special device of a dexter hand gules may be emblazoned on the shield as a canton in chief, as an inescutcheon. Although there is no certainty, some historians believe that the macabre term 'bloody hand' has reference to the blood shed by the native Catholic Irish who attempted to resist being dispossessed by King James's Protestant landlords. In 1625 King Charles I instituted the dignity of Baronets of Nova Scotia. The badge which unlike the Hand of Ulster is not displayed as a canton on the owner's shield but as a pendent beneath, embodies an inescutcheon of the arms of Scotland surmounted by an imperial crown on an escutcheon argent charged with a saltire azure.

SAMUEL PEPYS, ESQUIRE

'Sable, on a bend or between two horses' heads erased argent three fleur de lys sable. On a wreath of the colours a horse's head erased argent, bridled sable and ducally gorged. Mantling sable lined argent. Motto: MENS CUIUSQUE IS EST QUISQUE'. (Fig 254)

254

MENS CUIUSQUE IS EST QUISQUE

255

DOM MINA
INVS TIO
ILLV MEA

256

FLOREAT ETONA

257

ORANDO LABORANDO

The fame of Samuel Pepys as a diarist is too well established to need elaboration, and it is of his public life and great work for the British Navy that we must speak. The eldest son of a London tailor, Pepys began his career as a humble clerk in the Navy Office during the Commonwealth period under the Lord Protector. As a lad of sixteen he witnessed the execution of King Charles I outside the Banqueting House in Whitehall on 30 January 1648/49. At the Restoration he accompanied his cousin, Sir Edward Montague, to Holland to escort King Charles II and the Duke of York back to England. Montague was made a Knight of the Garter and created Earl of Sandwich, and though it was through his influence and patronage the Pepys's foot was set on the ladder leading to success, it was entirely through his own efforts that Pepys rose in the years that followed to that position of pre-eminence that entitles us to regard him as one of the greatest administrators England has ever had. It is no exaggeration to say that the reforms in naval matters that he effected laid the foundations of English naval supremacy in the eighteenth and nineteenth centuries. He overhauled the system of contracting, making it more difficult for fraudulent contractors to cheat with shoddy material; he was the first to introduce to the fleet naval chaplains responsible for the welfare of the ordinary seamen; and he did much to ensure that in future the officers should no longer obtain their appointments by patronage alone, but through training and merit.

In all this he was supported by his master, the Duke of York, as Lord High Admiral of England, and the King himself, both of whom appreciated Pepys's great merits. He was elected a Member of Parliament and on at least one occasion during the Popish Plot when the Commons were attacking what they called the misuse of the King's expenditure of public funds, he spoke strongly and to great effect in defence of the royal policy as regards the expenditure on the Navy. For his pains he suffered a term of imprisonment in the Tower, but was released to continue his great work. He was promoted to the rank of Secretary of the Admiralty, a position roughly equivalent to that of Minister of Defence today.

Pepys was one of the first Presidents of the Royal Society, that institution founded by Charles II that remain today the foremost scientific body in the world. He was also Master of Trinity House, the institution founded by Henry VIII which still exercises supreme authority over all lighthouses and lightships in British waters. On the accession of the Duke of York as James II in 1685, Pepys became one of the three or four most influential men in England; but when his master was forced to flee the country four years later, he preferred to retire into private life, feeling himself too long attached to his Stuart masters to serve William of Orange. His failing eyesight had caused him to abandon his famous Diary as far back as 1669, and for some years before his death in 1704 he was completely blind. In his will he left his library of books and the MS of the Diary to his old college of Magdalene at Cambridge.

BRITISH BROADCASTING CORPORATION

'Azure, a globe proper encircled by a band or surrounded by seven estoiles argent set in orle. On a wreath of the colours a lion passant or, langued gules, holding a winged thunderbolt proper. Supporters, on either side an eagle, wing elevated and addorsed proper, gorged with collars azure from which are suspended each a bugle horn stringed or. Motto: NATION SHALL SPEAK PEACE UNTO NATION. These arms for one of the best-known institutions in the world were granted in 1927. As one might expect, the various items of the achievement have symbolic significance. The gold circle round the globe signifies broadcast transmission, the thunderbolt represents electrical activity, while the supporter eagles with bugle horns represent swiftly borne proclamations.

This chapter may fittingly be concluded with some examples of arms and achievements granted to universities and schools. It is worth drawing attention to the fact that in the past not nearly enough care was taken by many such establishments to apply for official grants of arms, and in some cases the results have been disastrous. So called 'crests' and even arms have been reproduced on cap and blazer, writing paper and wall plaque, that are not only in bad taste, but defy the elementary rules of armorial blazon. It is much to be hoped that in future a proper approach will be made to the College of Arms, which one can be sure will be most sympathetically considered.

UNIVERSITY OF OXFORD

'Azure, between three open crowns or an open book proper, leathered gules, garnished and having on the dexter side seven seals also or, and inscribed with the words DOMINUS ILLUMINATIO MEA (Fig 225).

The Saxon town of Oxford or Oxenford was chosen as the site of the oldest British university very probably because it was not only situated at an important crossing place on the Thames linking the midlands with southern England, but also because ever since Robert D'Oiley, one of the Conqueror's barons, had built a castle there the town had been specially favoured by the Norman and first Plantagenet monarchs. It was Henry I (1100-1135) who built the royal palace of Beaumont (today commemorated by a street) and a hunting lodge at Woodstock. Richard the Lion Heart, in whose reign the first scholars from the older Paris University settled at Oxford, was born in Beaumont Palace. These early scholars, who were all churchmen, flocked to attend the lectures given by famous masters who came from France and Italy, and with the influx of the Franciscans some forty years later there were established a number of 'halls of residence' for the scholar clerks who came to attend the lectures and learn the art of disputation. There was as yet no corporate university in the later sense, and the scholars lived in these rented establishments under the authority of a master for disciplinary purposes. There were to be many disputes and even riots between 'town and gown', but royal and papal ordinances by the middle of the thirteenth century had secured a privileged position for the infant university, and established its independence from civic influence.

The same kind of development was taking place at Cambridge, whose university seems of have originated as the result of a migration of Oxford masters and scholars following a serious riot in the year 1209. The special favour shown to the two universities by Papal legates and kings can be explained by the fact that both Church and State looked to these establishments to produce that highly educated class of cleric that in medieval times was alone fitted to provide the statesmen and administrators necessary for good government.

As we have mentioned, the medieval process of education was by lecture and disputation. The scholar cleric entered the university at the age of fourteen or fifteen, and proceeded to the degree of Bachelor of Arts in his fourth year of residence. Thereafter he was licensed to give 'the less formal lectures'. After three more years he was admitted to the degree of Master of Arts when he went out into the world to serve either Church or the King's government. The highly prized degrees of Doctor of Theology, Medicine or Law required a further seven years of study, and were within the reach of very few. The curriculum for the degree of Bachelor was based on the seven liberal arts: grammar, rhetoric, logic, geometry, arithmetic, astronomy and music.

It is the college system that makes Oxford and Cambridge unique among universities today. Though the idea originated in Paris with its foundations of the Hotel Dieu and Sorbonne, it was not until the last quarter of the thirteenth century that the first Oxford and Cambridge colleges were founded. The honour of being the first is still the subject of dispute, but between 1280 and the end of the century University, Balliol and Merton were founded, to be followed in the next century by Exeter, Oriel and The Queen's colleges. In 1369 William of Wykeham, Bishop of Winchester and Chancellor to both Edward III and Richard II, founded New College and his school at Winchester. A century later another bishop of Winchester, William Waynflete, founded Magdalen College which was soon to be graced by the young Thomas Wolsey, who towards the end of his extraordinary and brilliant career, by dissolving the monastic foundations of St Frideswide and Oseney, set in order his plans for a new foundation to be called Cardinal's College. After Wolsey's fall the King himself established and endowed this great new foundation which became known as Christchurch. The College chapel, which was the beautiful priory church, in 1546 became the cathedral church of the newly created diocese of Oxford, and so it remains today.

The relation of college to university is always difficult to explain to the layman. In brief, each college - there are thirty-four in Oxford today - is self-governing and separately endowed. The studies, and all other activities of undergraduate members of the university, are controlled by the governing bodies of the colleges. These consist of a principal elected for life who bears the title Warden, President, Provost, Master or Principal; and a number of senior graduates who, apart from administering the affairs of their college, spend their time in lecturing and research. An important part of their work is taken up with giving 'tutorials' to the undergraduates, that is directing their studies and discussing their work in weekly private sessions. It is this 'tutorial system' that distinguishes the work of Oxford and Cambridge from that of other universities.

The university itself impinges only lightly on the lives of the undergraduates because their whole academic, social and sporting activities are practically contained within their colleges, the exception being 'public examinations' for the degree, and the degree ceremonies themselves. Nevertheless the colleges at Oxford and Cambridge in a corporate sense form the university, and it is from the ranks of their senior 'fellows' that the university officials, executive and legislating bodies are chosen. It would take far too long to describe them all, and we must be content with a brief mention of the most important. The chief executive officers are the Vice-Chancellor and the two Proctors, senior and junior. These are *ex officio* on all the more important committees, and are responsible for the running of university affairs. The Vice-Chancellor presides over Convocation which is an assembly of all members of the university holding the degree of master or doctor, whether they are resident or live and work elsewhere. This assembly meets seldom except for a token meeting for the conferring of degrees. The most important function of Convocation is to elect the Chancellor, who holds office for life. The Vice-Chancellor also presides over the two weekly sessions of Congregation. This is an assembly of college fellows, holders of faculty chairs, lecturers and so forth which meets to legislate; that is to pass university statutes concerned with finance, examinations, research and studies. Congregation is in fact the 'parliament' of the University. Finally, the Vice-Chancellor presides over the Hebdomadal Council which is in effect the 'cabinet' of University government.

Strangers to Oxford and Cambridge often ask which are the universtity buildings as distinct from those of the ancient colleges. At Oxford most of these are grouped between the High Street and the Broad, and include the Sheldonian Theatre where degrees are conferred, the Clarendon Buildings where the Proctors and University Registrar have their offices, the Bodleian Library which with its modern extension across the road has one of the greatest collections of books and MSS in the world, the ancient Convocation House where Parliament met in the reign of King Charles II, the Chancellor's Court adjoining, and the exquisite fifteenth-century building known as the Divinity School.

Reference has been made to the Chancellor of the University. In former centuries he was always a nobleman or bishop and exercised considerable authority over University affairs. In modern times his duties are practically confined to nominating the Vice-Chancellor on advice and occasionally presiding over Convocation. The Chancellor of Oxford is Mr Harold Macmillan.

ETON COLLEGE

'Sable, three lily flowers argent, 2 and 1, on a chief per pale azure and gules, a fleur de lys on the dexter and a lion passant guardant on the sinister side both or. Motto: FLOREAT ETONA (Fig 256).

In the arms of this famous English school both forms of the lily represent the Blessed Virgin to whom the College is dedicated. Founded by King Henry VI in 1440, Eton was granted arms by Letters Patent under the Great Seal on 1 January 1448. This is one of the very few examples of English arms granted directly by the sovereign, rather than by the usual practice whereby the Kings of Arms, under royal authority, grant arms having first received the warrant of the Earl Marshal to do so. The lion and fleur de lys shown betoken the special mark of royal favour in Eton's case. Although this saintly but ineffective monarch established his school across the river from Windsor for poor scholars, it became the fashion in the eighteenth century for the aristocracy and rich squirearchy to send their sons to Eton, with the result that in the following century it had acquired a reputation of exclusiveness. Many schools call themselves 'colleges' without justification, but Eton is governed by a Provost and Fellows who are ultimately responsible for financial administration and the appointment of the Headmaster. A former Provost of Eton was Dr M.R. James who acquired a public reputation beyond that usually accorded to eminent scholars through the excellent ghost stories that he wrote in his spare time, stories that are now regarded as classics.

RUGBY SCHOOL

'Azure, on a fess engrailed between three griffins' heads erased or, langued gules, a fleur de lys azure between two roses gules, barbed and seeded proper, all within a bordure or. On a wreath of the colours for crest a lion's gamb (forepaw) erased or, armed gules and charged with two roses in pale as on the escutcheon, grasping a branch of dates, the fruit in pods argent, leaved and slipped vert. Mantling of the colours. Motto: ORANDO LABORANDO (Fig 257).

The school was founded by the merchant, Lawrence Sherriff, in 1567. He held the post of purveyor of spices to Queen Elizabeth I, and this romantic-sounding appointment is symbolised in his blazon which, differenced by the bordure and the roses on the crest, was granted to his foundation. The griffin's head suggests the dragon-guarded treasures of the Levant, the branch of dates represents the spicery, while the Tudor roses and fleur de lys symbolise Sherriff's royal appointment.

Rugby School pursued an honourable but unexciting career as an Elizabethan grammar school until the appointment in 1829 as Headmaster of Dr Thomas Arnold, Fellow of Oriel College, Oxford. Readers of Thomas Hughes's classic *Tom Brown's Schooldays* will not need to be reminded of the rough and often brutal conditions existing in English boarding schools of the first half of the nineteenth century. It was Dr Arnold who led the field in instituting the reforms that completely changed the face of English school life. A man of courage, deep religious principle, and vision, he was not afraid to fight and overcome the most violent opposition. Within twenty years of his death there had been founded a number of new 'public schools' whose curriculum was based on the Christian religion, a modern academic syllabus, organised games, and the fostering of that code of behaviour that produced the 'officer and gentleman' class which with all its faults was to prove itself the backbone of Queen Victoria's vast empire. Today it is fashionable to sneer at 'class' and 'empire', but it is a fact of history that from these schools modelled on the reforms of Arnold of Rugby came most of the long line of pro-consuls, soldiers and administrators who were to give a large area of the world a greater era of peace based on the maintenance of law and justice than it had ever enjoyed before, or was to enjoy afterwards. On a less exalted plane, we may recall that it was Rugby School that gave its name to the famous game first played on the School Close. The circumstances are too well known to need repeating; but we may perhaps reflect that in the rough-and-tumble form of football then played, and so vividly described by Hughes, such an incident is much more creditable than it would have been in the modern game of Association football.

THE KING'S SCHOOL CANTERBURY

'Azure, on a cross argent a gothic text-letter 'x' surmounted by a text-letter 'i' sable. Motto: AGE DUM AGIS. (Fig 258)

258

259

These were the simple but curious arms borne by the medieval Priory of Canterbury. Education at the seat of the English primatial see has been continuous since its foundation by St. Augustine in AD 597. Until the Reformation this was in the hands of the Augustinian monks of the ancient priory. A unique feature of Canterbury's monastic constitution was that the Abbot was always the Archbishop, whose metropolitan and often political duties effectively removed him from immediate control, with the result that monastery affairs, including education, were in the hands of the Prior who was in effect the head of the community. When the priory was dissolved in 1539, the archiepiscopal see of course remained, the Prior and monks being replaced by a Dean and Chapter of residential canons to order the affairs of the cathedral. At the same time the King decided to transfer the existing scholars to a new foundation which became known as the King's School, in the charge of a master responsible to the Dean and Chapter. A transference of scholars from the town grammar school controlled by the medieval archbishops was also effected. Today the King's School ranks high in its record of scholarship and other activities among the public schools of Britain. Among the distinguished old boys stands forth the name of William Somerset Maugham. It is interesting to note that the school numbers among its buildings the medieval hospice in which it was customary for pilgrims to the shrine of Thomas Becket to pass the night at the end of their pilgrimage. Chaucer's pilgrims would have rested in this building. The school arms which, as we have noted, are those of the medieval priory, were granted by William Camden, the Elizabethan antiquary, in his capacity as Clarenceux King of Arms.

THE MERCHANT TAYLORS' SCHOOL

'Argent, a pavilion between two mantles imperial purpure, lined ermine, the pavilion garnished or, tent-staff also or; on a chief azure a lion passant guardant or. For crest, or a wreath argent and azure, a mount vert, thereon a lamb passant argent, all within a glory or. Mantling, argent lined gules. Supporters, on either side a camel or. Motto in chief [of the school]: HOMO PLANTAT HOMO IRRIGAT SED DEUS DAT INCREMENTUM. Motto in base [of the company]: CONCORDIA PARVAE RES CRESCUNT. (Fig 259).

The school is the property of, and is governed by, the Merchant Taylors' Company which was first incorporated in 1326. The original arms granted to the Company included certain religious emblems. The present arms were granted and the supporters added by Robert Cooke, Clarenceux King of Arms, in 1586. Originally a powerful medieval guild, the Merchant Taylors became an equally powerful and even richer trading company in Elizabethan times, and the various charges on the escutcheon and items of the achievement recall both past royal favours and the extent of the Company's trading area. The lion is a reminder that several monarchs had been Freemen of the Company, the tent and imperial mantles reflect the richness of the products the Merchant Taylors traded in, the supporter camels are a reminder not only of the fact that they were the animals of commerce in the East with which the Company traded, but the camel's hair was on scriptural authority the material for the clothes of St John Baptist, the patron saint of the Company, who is also represented by the lamb of the crest. It is interesting to note that a lamb bearing the banner of St George is the badge of St John's College, Oxford, also dedicated to the Baptist, and founded by Sir Thomas White, Lord Mayor of London and a member of the Merchant Taylor's Company.

260

261

MILL HILL SCHOOL

'Argent, on a cross quadrate gules an open book also argent. On a chief azure three martlets or. Motto: ET VIRTUEM ET MUSAS. (Fig 260)

The arms of this school were granted as recently as 1935, although as Mill Hill Grammar School it had been founded as far back as 1807. The present public school which was founded in 1895 incorporated the old grammar school. The martlets emblazoned in chief may symbolise the fact that Mill Hill held no endowment or property other than the land on which the school was built, putting us in mind that in was to trust to its 'wings of virtue and merit' to raise itself, and not to its legs, 'having little land to stand on'.

HARROW SCHOOL

'Azure, a lion rampant armed and langued gules, in dexter chief two arrows in saltire points downward tied in the centre with a bow and enfiled with a wreath of laurel all argent. As Badge, the wreath and arrow charge on the escutcheon. Motto in chief: STET FORTUNA DOMUS. Motto in base: DONORUM DEI DISPENSATIO FIDELIS. (Fig 261)

These are the arms of one of England's leading public schools, perhaps remembered today by the general public not so much for the scholastic and social position it has attained, as for the fact that Sir Winston Churchill was a pupil. Although the school was founded by John Lyon in the sixteenth century, no official arms were granted until 1929 when it had the distinction of receiving the grant at the hands of all three Kings of Arms. This may have been because a future Garter King of Arms, Sir Gerald Wollaston, in 1929 Norroy King of Arms, had himself been a pupil. Unlike other early founders, John Lyon does not seem to have taken the trouble to acquire arms, and was, therefore, unable to pass such on to his foundation. For the next four centuries Harrow seems to have made use of a number of unauthorised badges and crests. A curious feature of Harrow School arms is the absence of a crest which, of course, must always rest on a helmet. But Harrow can claim the distinction of being unique among leading public schools in possessing a badge. The lion charged on the escutcheon bears reference to the name of the founder, while the silver arrows recall the fact that an annual archery contest was formerly held at the school.

CHAPTER 9

Ecclesiastical Heraldry

The history of English ecclesiastical heraldry is more difficult to determine than that of its lay counterpart because one great source, the monastic foundations, was ruthlessly destroyed in King Henry VIII's dissolution between 1536 and 1540. Such examples as remain are found in surviving impressions of monastic seals, a few sculptured achievements on abbey ruins, and in a limited number of cases where charges on the shields of ancient monasteries or convents have been adopted by still flourishing boroughs which owe their arms in whole or in part to their associations in former times with pre-Reformation monastic foundations. Thus Reading University includes in its arms the three escallops of St James which are known to have been the arms of the great parliamentary abbey of Reading. The abbots of the larger and wealthier houses were regularly summoned to advise the king in Parliament. It is more with those pre-Reformation dioceses surviving today that we can speak with greater authority on medieval religious armory; and here we find that charges on the episcopal escutcheons were not invariably religious in their associations; for example, the see of Worcester is argent, charged with ten torteau. Another custom was for post-Reformation bishops to imitate many medieval bishops and abbots by impaling the official arms of the diocese (or abbey) with their personal arms on the sinister side. A very modern example of this is given by Boutell who illustrates the arms of Archbishop Fisher, former Archbishop of Canterbury:

> Argent, a fess wavy between three fleur de lys sable impaled by the arms of Canterbury, namely, azure, an episcopal staff in pale or, and ensigned with a cross patee argent surmounted of a pallium of the last charged with four crosses formee fitchee sable edged and fringed or. Two croziers in saltire behind the shield.

A feature peculiar to the arms of archbishops, with the single exception of York, is that they have charged on them the pallium. This was the divided strip of lamb's wool with an end piece in front conferred by the Pope on provincial archbishops to signify jurisdiction and authority within the province. It became customary to adorn the actual pallium, or pall, as it is often called, with sable crosses. The last Archbishop of Canterbury before the Reformation to have this papal pallium conferred on him was, ironically, Thomas Cranmer in 1533, who was, a few weeks later, in defiance of Pope Clement VII and the Catholic Church, to pronounce at Dunstable the divorce decree against Queen Catherine of Aragon. (The papal pallium was to be conferred once more on an Archbishop of Canterbury, but that was on Reginald Cardinal Pole during the short-lived Catholic reaction under Queen Mary Tudor.) What must appear to our age a flagrantly dishonest piece of double dealing was justified at the time on the compelling political grounds that Henry VIII's compliant new archbishop needed to be canonically consecrated and enthroned before he could act legally as archbishop . At that time the English Parliament had not passed the legislation which finally severed the Church in England from Rome, and Pope Clement did not wish to push to extremes the already strained relations between the two powers by refusing the pallium. Although Anglican archbishops no longer wear this insignia over their vestments, it remains as a symbol of the papal legatine authority they once enjoyed on their arms. To the archbishops of Canterbury remain two special privileges once granted by popes to their medieval predecessors: the authority to confer 'Lambeth' degrees, and the power to issue special marriage licences independent of the State.

The next point to note is that the clergy, being by canon law forbidden to take part in fighting, can display neither helmet nor crest above their arms. The ancient custom was, therefore, to ensign arms of religious with the mitre, for abbots and for bishops. This distinctive head dress of rank has taken different forms in different ages. In the earliest days of the Christian Church it was probably little more than a round, embroidered cap with a rising crown. By Norman times it had already developed the characteristic horns, but these were worn sideways. The next stage of development was the wearing of a mitre whose horns, now become triangular, rose from the crown front and back. This was the 'gothic' mitre in common use until the mid-sixteenth century, and the type generally emblazoned. One result of the Reformation was that the bishops of the newly established Church of England gave up the wearing of mitres and other vestments associated with the old Catholic mass; while the Catholic episcopate after the Council of Trent took to wearing a much taller mitre shaped rather like a tea-cosy. This they continued to wear until the wind of change which heralded the second Vatican Council brought about a reaction in favour of the old style of gothic vestments as well as mitres. By a strange quirk of irony, the Anglican bishops, who for four hundred years, had cast aside such a popish head dress, had already anticipated the Roman bishops by generally adopting the gothic mitre thirty or forty years earlier.

The next point to note is that the mitres of abbots, both as actually worn and as emblazoned, differ from those of bishops in respect of having no infulae. These are the two narrow fringed pieces of embroidered cloth pendent from the rear base of bishops' mitres.

Thirdly, it should be noted that the Roman Pontifical directs three types of mitre in Catholic ceremonial: the 'mitra pretiosa' or precious mitre which is of gold studded with jewels; the 'mitra aurifereta' or gold mitre which is of plain cloth of gold; and the 'mitra simplex' or white mitre. The first two are worn at various stages of pontifical high mass and certain other sacramental ceremonies, while the white mitre is worn only at requiem masses and other rites of the dead. In heraldry it is almost invariably the gold mitre that is emblazoned, for Anglican as well as for Catholic bishops and abbots. No distinction is made between the mitres of bishops and archbishops, since, strictly speaking, they are symbols of the holy Order rather than of ecclesiastical rank. The infulae are emblazoned draped on either side of the shield in the manner of mantling. Occasionally the mitre is found charged on the shield itself, as in the case of the medieval See of Llandaff, in those days within the province of Canterbury.

One interesting exception to the rule is to be found in the arms of the See of Durham which depict a ducal coronet resting on the shield and a bishop's mitre issuing therefrom. The heraldic significance of this is that occupants of this see were formerly 'prince-bishops' enjoying palatinate or temporal jurisdiction over most of the county of Durham.

The emblem of rank displayed in the arms of a provincial archbishop is the episcopal staff 'in pale' behind the shield. In the case of Canterbury and York, this represents the actual metropolitan or provincial cross carried before these prelates in their provinces to signify jurisdiction. According to ancient church law, a metropolitan archbishop's cross should be double-traversed (two bars to the cross), and so it has been emblazoned in the arms used by the Catholic archdiocese of Westminster (see below).

We might also note that strictly speaking all diocesan bishops should emblazon behind their shields two croziers in saltire. The crozier or pastoral staff is derived from the shepherd's crook and represents the bishop's authority according to the Scripture as a shepherd over his flock. One interesting distinction between the crozier of a bishop and that of an abbot is that the former should curl outwards, signifying the bishop's external authority over his territorial diocese, while the latter curls inwards, signifying the limited authority of the abbot over his community. This rule does not seem to be very ancient - the elaborately carved crozier of William of Wykeham, Bishop of Winchester at the end of the fourteenth century, now preserved at his foundation of New College, Oxford, shows no such outward curl; while the crozier of Stephen Fox, also Bishop of Winchester and Lord Privy Seal to Kings Henry VII and VIII one hundred years later, shows the outward curl unmistakably.

It remains to set forth briefly the history of Roman Catholic diocesan arms in England and Wales. The last pre-Reformation prelate, Thomas Goldwell, Bishop of St Asaph, died in exile in 1585. For the next 265 years English Catholics were governed by archpriests, and then by 'Vicars Apostolic'. Until the beginning of the eighteenth century English Roman Catholics suffered severe persecution under the penal laws passed by Elizabethan Parliaments, and they did not obtain complete toleration and political equality until the passing of the Catholic Emancipation Act in 1829. When Pope Pius IX restored the English Catholic hierarchy in 1850, he fixed the Metropolitan See at Westminster, and made provision for the appointment of twelve suffragan bishops. Under the terms of the Ecclesiastical Title Act (14 and 15 Vic c.60) passed by a strongly Protestant Parliament, no Roman Catholic bishop could establish his see in the cathedral city of any Church of England diocesan bishop existing at that time, nor could he bear the title of any Anglican diocese. One of the results of this decision was that new arms had to be found for these new Catholic dioceses. When the College of Arms was approached the discovery was made that no grants of arms could be made because, unlike the Established Church, the new Catholic sees could not be recognised in law. In the event the Catholic bishops assumed arms for their sees, impaling them with their own personal arms. Later an attempt was made to have papal grants of arms officially recognised; but while the College of Arms was willing to recognise that the Pope as *Fons Honorum* (sovereign source of honours) was entitled to bestow arms on his subjects, papal writ did not run in England.

This is not the time or place to describe in detail all the arms of the English Catholic dioceses; but we may note those of the Metropolitan See of Westminster, and also the Catholic fashion of ensigning frequently diocesan arms with the ecclesiastical hat rather than with the mitre.

ARCHDIOCESE OF WESTMINSTER

'Gules, an episcopal staff in pale or ensigned with a cross patee also or, surmounted of a pallium argent charged with four crosses formee fitchy sable fringed and edged or. A provincial cross double-barred or in pale behind the shield. These arms ensigned of a Cardinal's Hat garnished with thirty tassels gules.' (By tradition the Pope customarily bestows the Red Hat on new archbishops of Westminster at the first Consistory held after enthronement. Until created a cardinal an archbishop would ensign his arms with the archbishop's hat.)

It will be noticed that with the exception of hat and provincial cross these arms are the arms of the archdiocese of Canterbury differenced. They were in fact granted by Pope Leo XIII by decree in the year 1894, the azure field of Canterbury being changed to red to signify the blood shed for their Faith by the English Catholic martyrs.

THE ECCLESIASTICAL HAT

In the Roman Church hats of rank are carefully graded in colour and number of tassels, and this is reflected in armorial bearings. The custom seems to have originated with Pope Innocent IV (1243-1254), who was the first to bestow on members of the Sacred College of Cardinals as a supreme emblem of rank large red hats with rows of pendent tassels. The word 'cardinal' means 'a hinge', and the significance is apparent when it is remembered that since the tenth century the supreme office of these men had been to elect the new pope, and that in the Middle Ages the occupant of the Chair of St Peter wielded enormous power, both sprirtually and politically. Today all the cardinals are devout hard-working churchmen in at least bishop's orders; but until the reforms of the Council of Trent in the mid-sixteenth century it was not uncommon to find laymen wearing the red hat, or at most receiving only minor orders which did not restrict them in secular activities. Men like Cesare Borgia, immersed in Italian politics and then resigning his cardinalate to lead the life of a conquering general, spring to mind. Even the saintly Reginald, Cardinal Pole, who became the last Catholic Archbishop of Canterbury, received the major orders of priest and bishop less than one week before he was enthroned in Canterbury Cathedral in 1554. In modern times the members of the Sacred College are either the occupants of provincial sees in all parts of the world, or members of the Curia in Rome (prefects of the various consistorial bodies that govern under the Pope the Roman Catholic Church).

Until the sixteenth century the cardinals customarily wore their red hats on ceremonial occasions, or hung them on their backs by the tassel cords tied across the breast. The custom had changed, it seems, when Thomas Wolsey was raised to the purple by Pope Leo X in 1515 because this remarkable man, already Archbishop of York and High Chancellor of England, had the papal messenger bringing the hat from Rome stopped before he could enter London, to give time to organise one of the magnificent processions for which Wolsey was famous. The red hat was solemnly borne in procession to Westminster Abbey and placed on the altar. Today it would be impossible for a cardinal to wear his hat, because it has long lost its crown. Measuring over two feet in diameter, it is momentarily placed on the new cardinal's head at one of the ceremonies of the consistory of creation, and then some time later borne in procession before the prelate as he enters his cathedral. It is not seen again until it is placed on his coffin at the funeral rites. Finally, the hat is hung in perpetuity over the tomb. The number and nature of the tassels of cardinals' and other ecclesiastical hats seems to have varied at different periods of history. The numbers accorded to the different ranks of the hierarchy today were fixed by the Sacred Congregation of Rites in 1832, and are faithfully reproduced in the armorial bearings of Roman Catholic sees:

Rank	Colour of Hat	Number of tassels
Cardinals	Red	30; 15 each side in 5 rows of 1, 2, 3, 4, and 5
Patriarchs	Green	As for cardinals
Archbishops	Green	20; 10 each side
Bishops	Green	12; 6 each side
Protonotaries Apostolic Superiors	Violet	12; 6 each side (colour red)
General	Black	12; 6 each side
Canons	Black	6; 3 each side
Priests	Black	4; 2 each side.

CHAPTER 10

Arms of Heiresses, and Hatchments

THE FEMALE LOZENGE

The rules governing blazon have always insisted that the arms of unmarried women and widows must be displayed not on a shield but on a lozenge. When an heiress marries, her arms are either placed on her husband's shield on an inescutcheon of pretence, or simply impaled with his, and the lozenge disappears. But when a peeress in her own right marries a commoner, she cannot confer rank upon her husband, so he is not allowed to incorporate the coronet and supporters of her peerage in his own achievement. The arms of the alliance are therefore marshalled as follows. The peeress's arms are placed in the centre of her husband's in an inescutcheon of pretence surmounted by the coronet of her degree. They are repeated on a lozenge together with her supporters and coronet, the achievement being placed on the sinister side of that of her husband. The arms of heiresses are of course inherited by their heirs in law; but those of unmarried women and widows, not being heiresses, die with them.

FUNERAL HATCHMENTS

One of the principal sources of knowledge of early heraldic art is the display of armorial bearings in marble and stone over cathedral and parish church tombs of long-dead lords and knights. In an age far less materialistic than our own, the transitory nature of life on earth was a thought never far from men's minds, and the comforting pomp of ceremonies in honour of the dead did not disappear with requiem masses for the souls of the departed at the time of the Reformation. In particular in England the new society created by the Tudor monarchs out of the ruins of monasticism was paradoxically proud to show its connection with the great families of the past, and the occasion of a funeral with the ceremonial trappings still customary afforded just such an opportunity. With the passing years Puritan influence, it is true, imposed severe restrictions on all religious ceremonial; but after the exterior gloom of the Commonwealth the Restoration gentry, as proudly conscious of their armigerous past as their ancestors, found a new way to satisfy their pride of family and social aspirations. This was the 'funeral hatchment', which was introduced in the middle of the seventeenth century and continued to be popular for nearly two hundred years.

This hatchment took the form of a diamond-shaped (lozenged) board or framed piece of canvas on which were emblazoned in brilliant colours the arms of the deceased person. No doubt the idea suggested itself from the custom of carrying ceremonial shields at the funerals of an earlier age. The hatchment, which varies in size up to about 5ft 6in in height, was, immediately on the death of the owner, set up over the entrance to his house to remain there for one year, the customary period of mourning. At the end of that time it was taken to the church of burial and set up in perpetuity over the tomb, if that were in the body of the church, or fastened to a convenient wall if the grave were in the churchyard. Before setting forth the customs governing the emblazoning of hatchments we may add a note of historic interest. This seventeenth- and eighteenth-century fashion was responsible for a serious and prolonged dispute between the heraldic painters and the College of Arms. This seems to have come about because the great demand for funeral hatchments often resulted in the painters themselves being consulted by the relatives of the deceased with regard to blazon and design. This practice was of course both cheaper and speedier than an approach to the heralds themselves; but it was illegal, and more often than not resulted in serious technical and historical errors creeping in. The dispute was not resolved until several lengthy law-suits had run their course.

262

263

264

265

Hatchment of Unmarried Man: Background all black; shield (not impaled), crest, helmet and mantling (Fig 262).

Hatchment of Married Man with Wife living: Background dexter side only black (behind husband's arms); shield impaled (husband's arms dexter, wife's arms sinister), crest helmet and mantling (Fig 263).

Hatchment of Widower: Background all black; shield impaled (husband's arms dexter, wife's arms sinister); crest, helmet and mantling (Fig 264).

Hatchment of Married Man with Second Wife living: Background black behind arms of husband and first wife; shield impaled, sinister side parted per fess to display arms of both wives (Fig 265).

Hatchment of Married Woman with Husband still living: Background black sinister side only (behind deceased wife's arms); shield impaled, crest helmet and mantling (Fig 266).

Hatchment of Widow: Background all black; lozenge impaled, no crest, helmet or mantling (Fig 267).

Hatchment of Unmarried Woman: Background all black; lozenge with simple arms (not impaled), no crest, helmet or mantling (Fig 268).

(The lozenge of the last two hatchments conform to the rules of blazon for widows and unmarried women.)

CHAPTER 11

The Seal

I

In any study of heraldry the seal must occupy a distinguished position, not only for the beauty of the craftsmanship revealed in examples surviving from many centuries, but also because the devices engraved on early seals constitute an important source for historians. It is not easy to determine exactly when the fashion of sealing important documents began. There is reason to suppose it was not unknown to the ancient world, and that Egyptians, Babylonians and Assyrians used some sort of seal. In the West we have no evidence of its use until the seventh century of the Christian era when we hear of papal edicts being sealed with the leaden 'bulla', an early type of seal which took its name from the little metal box formerly hung round the necks of well-born Roman children which contained a charm to protect them from harm. This is, of course, the origin of the term 'Papal Bull' applied to official edicts of the Popes. The earliest example of a royal seal is that of the Holy Roman Emperor Otto III who died in the year 1002. It showed the Emperor enthroned with the emblems of royalty and, setting a fashion adopted by later emperors and kings or western Europe, became known as the 'Seal of Majesty'.

The first English monarch to make official use of a seal was Edward the Confessor. The Conqueror as Duke of Normandy had a seal depicting him on horseback holding the ducal sword. When he became King William I he continued to use the Duchy seal, but, for greater security, had the reverse side of the metal matrix engraved as a Seal of Majesty, with his portrait enthroned holding sword and sceptre. This was described as the 'Counterseal'. The Conqueror's successors reversed this so that the Seal of Majesty became the obverse, while the reverse was used for some other device. Until the thirteenth century the use of seals was confined to kings, the feudal nobility and the higher clergy attending the king's court. But from the thirteenth century all sorts of people began to make use of this convenient way of authenticating their official documents, and before long the engravers were being kept busy fashioning in silver and in bronze the devices and arms of monasteries, universities, civic corporations and merchant guilds. In an age when few people were able to read or write and signatures might be forged undetected, the wax impressions of seals provided a guarantee of authenticity.

Important persons employed more than one seal. Bishops, for example, used as many as four: the 'seal of dignity', a seal for current business affairs known as the *sigellum ad causas,* a private seal, and a signet ring. The king also had several seals, and because three great departments of government were to evolve when eventually separation from the domestic household occurred, it will be as well to examine these three seals in some detail.

THE GREAT SEAL

The Norman King Henry I (1110-1135) was the first English monarch to organise departments of government out of the royal household. The Exchequer Board was one of his successful creations; the Department of the Chapel was another, and it derived its name from the fact that according to custom it was staffed by royal chaplains, the only members of the King's household capable of reading and writing. The work of this department was to prepare and issue the royal writs addressed to the King's sheriffs and other officials. In those days royal households led a communal life in the great hall of the king's palace, and it was soon found necessary to secure the peaceful conditions necessary for the despatch of this important work by separating the chaplains or clerks from the rest of the household by a screen known in the official Latin of the day as the *Cancella*. The King had placed these clerks in the charge of a great nobleman (usually a bishop) without whose authority the King's seal could not be impressed. It was thus but a short step to this official acquiring the title of *Cancellarius,* or *Chancellor*. Because all important state documents were required to be 'passed under the Great Seal', the Chancellor's position rose in importance until he ranked second only to the Lord Treasurer. Indeed, when the holder of this office was a man of outstanding ability he acquired an influence in political matters which made him in effect first or 'prime' minister. Among the great holders of this office have been Thomas Becket, Archbishop of Canterbury; Thomas Wolsey, Cardinal and Archbishop of York; Sir Thomas More; Stephen Gardiner, Bishop of Winchester in Queen Mary Tudor's reign; Francis Bacon, Lord Verulam; Anthony Ashley Cooper, first Earl of Shaftesbury; and Sir Edward Hyde, Earl of Clarendon. By Wolsey's time the Chancellor's department had become a court of equity, and the Chancellor's work was largely taken up with presiding over the work of this court. But because he still retained charge of the Great Seal, which on ceremonial occasions was carried before him in an elaborately embroidered silk purse, he was always a minister of the monarch and 'Keeper of the King's Conscience', being his mouthpiece in Parliament which he opened and prorogued or dissolved in the King's name, and to which he spoke the King's will. With the development of constitutional government the Chancellor's political influence declined; but some relics of his once extensive power still remain. The Lord Chancellor in modern times is always a member of the Cabinet, he presides over sessions of the House of Lords, and he presides as a judge over the judicial functions of the House of Lords and the Judicial Committee of the Privy Council. He is also responsible for the appointment of all High Court judges (except the Lord Chief Justice), county court judges and Queen's Counsel, and can dismiss metropolitan magistrates and justices of the peace.

It followed that the Great Seal itself was regarded as an object of very great importance. Constitutionally our forefathers came to believe that no important act of government could be carried out in its absence. A heavy object at one time cast in silver, it was engraved on the obverse side with the image of the reigning monarch enthroned in majesty, and on the counterseal with the royal arms of England. A new seal was customarily made for each reign, the old seal being ceremonially broken on the demise of the Crown. So important was popular regard for this emblem of state that successive monarchs always took great care over the bestowing of its guardianship, and when travelling abroad or in times of crisis often insisted on taking it with them for fear that such a potentially powerful political weapon might fall into the wrong hands. The Great Seal of Richard I Coeur de Lion went through a number of exciting adventures when that much-travelled monarch was busying himself with Crusading matters. To quote Dr A.L. Poole, writing in the *Oxford History of England,*

> It was shipwrecked off Cyprus with the King's seal-bearer, Roger Malchiel, in April, 1191, but was recovered when Roger's body was washed ashore; on the King's return from Palestine it fell into the hands of Leopold of Austria who possibly handed it over to the King's brother, John, who may have used it for his own purposes. Richard regained possession of it in 1193, and shortly after a new seal was made, but it was not taken into use till the spring of 1198.

As the King died the following year, this second seal must have had a short life, for the next monarch, Richard's brother, had a new one made, according to custom. It was this new seal that has become perhaps the most famous of all the Great Seals of the Realm because it must have been used to seal Magna Carta, and the impression in green wax of King John enthroned in majesty may still be seen attached to the British Museum copy.

In the troubled days of the Wars of the Roses Lancastrian and Yorkist kings carefully guarded their seals. Richard III, the last Plantagenet king, sent to Westminster on order to his Chancellor to send the Great Seal to him at Nottingham Castle where he was spending the summer of 1485 waiting for the expected invasion of Henry Tudor. No doubt the King was anxious lest this symbol of authority should fall into the hands of his enemies in London. It is not known if he took it into battle, to be found after Bosworth like his crown under a hawthorn bush. The last English king to exercise personal political power held similar views regarding the power of the seal. King James II on his flight to France in 1688 dropped his Great Seal over the side of his boat in the river Thames, hoping, no doubt, that in his absence from the kingdom its loss would confound the government of his enemies; but as it was recovered next day by a fisherman, we shall never know to what extent constitutionally its loss might have embarrassed the Lords of the Convention. After this a more down-to-earth attitude became the fashion, doubtless because with the breaking of the direct line of succession, 'sacredness' departed from the monarchy. Indeed, under the Hanoverians attitudes regarding the Great Seal seem to have swung to the opposite extreme, as witness a Lord Chancellor of 150 years later who took the Seal of the day on holiday with him to Scotland and used it to make girdle cakes! Such extreme iconoclasm was, however, too much for even his Hanoverian master, and King William IV was exceedingly angry when it was reported to him.

As we have mentioned, the Great Seal used to be carried before the

Chancellor in procession in a great silk purse. Although the purse still figures largely in ceremonies with which the Lord Chancellor is associated, it is always empty, very possibly because, according to legend, an eighteenth-century holder of the office by accident dropped it on his foot, causing him to break a bone of his toe. Today new parliaments are still summoned by writ under the Great Seal, creations of peerages are issued under its impression, and important treaties require its impress. But this ancient emblem of lawful government remains locked in a small chamber in the Victoria Tower of the House of Lords.

THE PRIVY SEAL

The Privy or private Seal seems to have made its first appearance late in the reign of King John when that much frustrated monarch, checkmated by the barons, who now controlled the Great Seal, over his extra-legal activities, decided to issue his writs under the authority of a private seal. In matters of domestic economy his successors found it convenient to copy this practice, and a new department of the household was created, looked after by clerks of the King's Chamber. But early in the fourteenth century the Privy Seal passed under the control of a committee of barons named the Lords Ordainers who feared the unconstitutional use of this instrument of government by King Edward II (1307-1327), whose character, unfortunately, inclined him to bestow political rewards on favourites with homosexual tendencies. By way of revenge the King sought to transfer the Privy Seal's authority to the Wardrobe, a department originally concerned with purely domestic matters. To some extent he and his successors were successful, but the Privy Seal became a department of state in 1313 when the barons appointed a Lord Keeper of this Seal with a professional body of clerks. The holder of this office ranked after the Lord Chancellor and the Lord Treasurer. The first Keeper to be named Lord Privy Seal was Richard Foxe, Bishop of Winchester and trusted counsellor of Henry VII and Henry VIII for the early years of the latter's reign. The importance of this office declined when Foxe resigned and his protége Wolsey, as Lord Chancellor, became the King's chief minister; but after Wolsey's fall Thomas Cromwell held the Privy Seal for a short time at the end of his career when he had already established his reputation as perhaps the greatest administrator England had ever had. Today the office of Lord Privy Seal is always given to a leading member of the government, although his political duties may be very different from those of earlier holders of this office.

THE SIGNET AND THE SECRETARYSHIP

It was King Richard II (1377-1399) who created the office of the Signet. The ring seal had been used for centuries by monarchs and other notables to seal personal and private communications. King Richard's innovation was the result of the loss of royal control over the Privy Seal and Wardrobe departments, but he did not appoint a nobleman or a bishop over the new department, being content that its administration should be in the hands of royal clerks presided over by a secretary. It was not until 1530 that the office of the Signet saw any change in its status, and then it was because the secretaryship was bestowed upon Thomas Cromwell, the King's new chief minister, who transformed this modest office into one of the most powerful. In Cromwell's hands the Signet was made the key office of Henry VIII's government to coordinate and secure the smooth running of all other departments of state. So successful was the King's Secretary that after his death the King appointed a second Secretary, and for the next two hundred years the entire work of government passed through the hands of one or other of the two Secretaries of State. Among those statesmen who have held this office and have left their mark on history are William Cecil, Lord Burghley; his son, Robert Cecil, Earl of Salisbury; Sir Edward Nicholas; Sir Henry Coventry, the friend of Pepys; Sydney Godolphin; Robert Harley, Earl of Oxford; Henry St John, Viscount Bolingbroke; and William Pitt, Earl of Chatham. The two Secretaries continued to function, one for the southern department of the realm and the other for the northern department, until the end of the eighteenth century; but by about 1780 government had become more complex, and there were now several more secretaryships. In modern times all those cabinet ministers who hold Secretaryships of State can in a real sense be said to have derived their offices from the old Signet office. And each has a 'Seal of Office' which he surrenders to the Queen on relinquishing his appointment. Moreover, every 'order' published by the minister under authority of Act of Parliament requires the impression of his seal before it can become mandatory.

II

Such is the history of the royal seals of England. We have noted that it was not until the thirteenth century that the fashion spread to other ranks and classes of society, and it was in this century that there began the custom of engraving on the counterseal (sometimes the obverse only) the arms of the owner. The metal seal being a much more durable object than parchment and perhaps less expendable than actual war shields, it is not surprising that our knowledge of certain ancient arms is derived from surviving examples of the seal engraver's art. In Chapter 2 reference was made to the probable origin of the custom of adding supporters to arms. It was suggested that the engraver, faced with the problem of filling up the blank spaces created by imposing a square or triangular shield on a round surface, provided embellishment in this form. A study of very ancient shields reveals that they did not always design two creatures dexter and sinister to support the shield. A seal of 1316, that of the Duke of Normandy, bears the arms of ancient France with a border gules between two lions rampant *away* from the shield and an eagle displayed above. The seal of Yolande de Flandres, Countess of Bar in 1340, bears her arms with the blank spaces filled with the symbols of the four Evangelists. The seal of a French lady in 1311 shows the lady herself bearing in one hand a shield emblazoned with her husband's arms, and in the other a shield with her own arms. Two of the earliest seals are those of Boleslas III, King of Poland, and of Florent, Count of Hainault. The former, dating from 1255, shows an armed knight holding a shield emblazoned with the Polish eagle, while the latter, from the year 1283, depicts a knight in chain mail supporting a shield charged with a lion impaling an eagle dimidiated. The seal of the magnificent fifteenth-century Dukes of Burgundy depicted a lion sejant helmeted and crested bearing on the breast the arms of Burgundy between three other shields. This was the official seal of Duke Philip the Good (1417-1467), founder of the Order of the Golden Fleece, and of his son Charles the Rash (1467-1477), the last of the independent dukes, who married Margaret Plantagenet, sister of King Edward IV of England. Coming nearer home, the seal of Archibald, fourth Earl of Douglas, in 1418 shows the shield of the Douglas arms held in the dexter hand of an erect savage who holds also in the same hand a club, and in the sinister hand a helmet. In England the seal of Henry Percy, First Earl of Northumberland, shows the Percy arms (azure, five fusils conjoined in fess or) supported by a knight who stands behind the shield.

CHAPTER 12

The Badge

Many people loosely use the term 'badge' to describe any device appearing in heraldic form. They speak of a school or college blazer badge, though crest or escutcheon may actually be thereon emblazoned. The heraldic badge is something quite different in form as well as in origin. We shall be describing and illustrating one or two historic badges below.

The badge seems to have originated as a device worn on the livery of the armed retainers of the feudal lord. It was obviously advantageous in the mêlée of a battle for the men to be able to recognise one another and their lord. Moreover, custom and law prevented the display of personal arms on retainers. The potential power of such symbols so worn seems to have been recognised by that astute monarch, Henry VII, who put an end to the old practice by his famous Statute of Maintenance and Livery. Thereafter, the badge survived only as a symbol of status to decorate silver plates, cups and spoons of an armigerous-minded rising middle class, and the only survival of its feudal origins is in the signboards of a few old inns whose original landlords had started life as feudal tenants. Later developments included the practice of detaching the crest from an achievement to employ it as a badge, though this does not appear to have received authority from the College of Arms. In modern times badges are correctly displayed on military standards (see Chapter 13), panels of coaches and motor cars, writing paper and caps both military and educational. The badges illustrated below have played some part in British history, and a brief account of each is appended.

Bear and Ragged Staff (Beauchamp Earls of Warwick) This badge was passed on by inheritance to the Neville earls in the mid-fifteenth century, and during the Wars of the Roses was much in evidence on the livery of the King-Maker's retainers. When in the following century John Dudley, Lord de Lisle, was created Earl of Warwick, he may have adopted the Beauchamp badge, but as shortly after he persuaded the young Edward VI to raise him to the new dukedom of Northumberland, he cannot have had much use for it. On the other hand, after Queen Elizabeth had created her favourite, Robert Dudley, Earl of Leicester, we have evidence that he made frequent use of the Bear and Ragged Staff; though he justified its use by virtue of his possession of Kenilworth Castle, a principal seat of the old Warwick family which the Queen had also bestowed on him. It remains today a charge on the arms of the county of Warwick. (See Fig 104)

Estoile (John de Vere, Twelfth Earl of Oxford) The de Vere earls of Oxford, one of the most ancient of the noble houses of England, have left their mark on the history of the country. An early de Vere earl was knighted by Simon De Montfort before the battle of Lewes in 1264 which established the temporary ascendency of the baronage over King Henry III. A hundred and thirty years later Robert de Vere, the life-long friend of Richard II, leading the royal forces, was defeated at Radcot Bridge and sent into exile. In the next century the de Veres supported the Lancastrians against the Yorkists, and John, the twelfth Earl, marched with the King-Maker Earl of Warwick against Edward IV and the Yorkist army at Barnet in 1471. It was on this occasion, as will be related below, that a tragic mistake in identifying badges played a part in altering the course of history. The thirteenth Earl was more fortunate, and was rewarded for his loyalty to Henry Tudor with the posts of Lord High Admiral and Constable of the Tower. A hundred years later the Elizabethan de Vere, Earl of Oxford, had the distinction of being the patron of Shakespeare. The direct line and the peerage came to an end in the seventeenth century. (Fig 269)

269   270

Sun in Splendour (King Edward IV) This badge was the personal cognizance of the Yorkist king, and was worn on the livery of his troops in the bloody battles of the civil war that waged for thirty years between the Houses of York and Lancaster. Reference has been made to the tragic mistake in badges that played some part in deciding the outcome of the battle of Barnet. In the early morning mist of that Easter morning when the two armies clashed, the Earl of Warwick's Lancastrian troops mistook the royal 'Sun in Splendour' for the Star badge of the retainers of the Earl of Oxford who was commanding a wing of the Lancastrian army. In the event the Yorkists won a decisive victory, King Edward was restored to his throne, the Earl of Warwick was slain, and the Earl of Oxford fled into exile. (Fig 270)

Portcullis (Beaufort family) The first Tudor king was descended through his mother, the Lady Margaret Beaufort, from John Beaufort, son of John of Gaunt by his third marriage. Thus after 1485 the Beaufort Portcullis badge became a royal badge. It still figures on the Collar of 'SS' worn by the Lord Chief Justice and other officers of state, as it did once on the collar of John of Gaunt who was Lord High Steward. Until recently this device figured also on the reverse of the British threepenny bit. It also forms a gilt motive stamped on the green benches and Speaker's Chair in the House of Commons Chamber. (See Fig 142)

CHAPTER 13

Banners of Arms, Standards and Flags

There has been and still remains much confusion in the popular mind concerning banners, standards and flags. To many people the word 'banner' conjures up pictures of a rectangular piece of cloth embroidered with words or symbols, which is fixed to a pole and carried in church processions or by persons protesting about something. By a similar misconception the banner is often referred to as a 'standard', as when people speak of the 'Royal Standard' when they ought to speak of the 'Royal Banner'. Possibly both banner and standard had their prototype in the Roman legionary standard, that tall staff surmounted by the Roman Eagle and bearing round discs to record battle honours. In much the same way two thousand years later the Queen's regiments of Guards on great ceremonial occasions march behind their battle emblazoned 'colours'. The modern flag is also derived from the banner rather than from the standard, but we shall be discussing this later.

THE BANNER OF ARMS

The medieval banner was either square in shape or oblong, greater in depth than breadth. It was charged with the arms of the owner, but without crest, supporters or any other device. It was carried before or immediately after the lord on ceremonial occasions; but it was not carried into battle, as is sometimes falsely represented. The only possible exception may have been in the case of the banner of the sovereign or royal prince leading an army, when there would be military need for the commander-in-chief to be recognised by his knights and soldiers in the confused fury of the fighting. One must remember that we are speaking of the days when it was customary for kings personally to lead their armies into battle. Sir Laurence Olivier, following Shakespeare, was therefore probably historically within his rights to show the banners of England and St George borne before him in the Agincourt scenes of his famous film version of *Henry V*. The use of the banner was not confined to the land. It became the custom to emblazon sails with the arms of lords and knights holding command at sea. In the Middle Ages there was no professional navy, battles at sea being fought by soldiers crowded on to the ordinary merchant ships of the day pressed into service for a particular cause. The duties of the ship master and sailors were to navigate and bring their ships alongside or near enough to the enemy either to ram or board them, when the soldiers and fighting knights took over the business of warfare. Thus in the mêlée of a sea fight, as on land, emblazoned sails would play their part.

It was, however, on the great ceremonial occasions that the banner came into its own, particularly on the occasion or a coronation. Since the Conqueror was crowned King of England on Christmas Day in the year 1066, thirty-five times have the lieges gathered within the walls of the ancient abbey to render homage to their lord king or queen, and from at least the coronation of Edward II, when the famous Coronation Chair was first used, each feudal lord had his own banner emblazoned with his personal arms borne before him. In modern times only what we may call the 'national' banners of the three kingdoms (see below) are carried in procession. It is perhaps of interest that in 1902 King Edward VII conferred the privilege of carrying the Banner of England on Sir Henry Dymoke, Lord of the Manor of Scrivelsby in the county of Lincolnshire, whose ancestors since 1327 had possessed the right as King's Champion to ride in full armour into Westminster Hall at the Coronation Banquet to throw down the gauntlet to challenge to mortal combat any who should dispute the right of the newly crowned monarch to reign. The Dymokes of Scrivelsby had not exercised this right since the coronation of George IV in 1821, at the last Coronation Banquet ever to be held. Something of the ancient splendour of banner display has survived also in the pageantry attending to this day the installation ceremonies of the great orders of chivalry, and in St George's Chapel, Windsor, in St Giles's Cathedral, Edinburgh, and in the Henry VII Chapel, Westminster, and at ceremonies of the Most Venerable Order of the Hospital of St John of Jerusalem at the Grand Priory Church, Clerkenwell, and elsewhere, the visitor may feast his eyes on the serried ranks of the emblazoned banners of the Knights hung high above the carved stalls amidst all the splendour of gothic architecture. Many of the older banners were not square as are the ceremonial banners hung in the chapels, but oblong. In these latter cases the correct way to fly them is to attach the banner to its staff with the longer side upright, the only position that permits the blazon, which occupied the whole area, to be properly displayed. See Fig 271.

271

THE STANDARD

The medieval standard was the long, tapering flag under which the feudal lord mustered his retainers, and which was then borne before him to serve as a rallying point and as an encouragement to the troops. After the creation of a standing army by Henry VIII it does not seem to have been carried into battle, being used for purely ceremonial purposes. An important distinction to be made between the standard and the banner is that the former was never emblazoned with the arms of the owner. This rule, however, has been abrogated in modern times. The essential characteristics of the medieval standard may be set forth as follows:

1   In form long and tapering, its length was in proportion to the rank of its owner. The narrow end furthest from the mast was often swallow-tailed or V-shaped.
2   Except when the standard bore a royal device it carried in a panel set nearest to the mast the cross of St George.
3   It bore two tinctures, parted fess-wise, and was also fringed with a border gobony of two tinctures which were usually the livery colours of the owner.
4   The standard was also charged with representation of the owner's badge; sometimes also the motto was added bend-wise across the fly.

In modern times, says Boutell, standards charged with badges may be granted to any armigerous persons, and may also be charged with the owner's arms emblazoned in a panel next to the mast. See Fig 272.

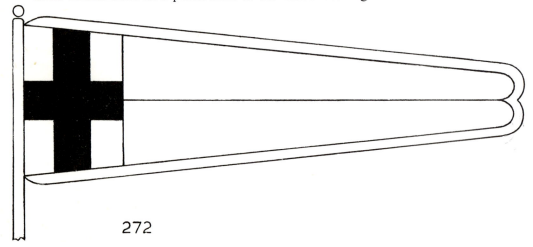

272

THE FLAG

The *Shorter Oxford Dictionary* defines the flag as a 'piece of bunting or other material, usually oblong or square, attached by one edge to staff or halyard and used as standard, ensign or signal'. In attempting to define the flag as distinct from the banner or any similar piece of blazon this definition is not exactly helpful. One possible solution would be to qualify the dictionary definition by describing the flag as an emblazoned piece of bunting of recognisable shape, flown on staff or halyard for all purposes other than those exclusive to banner or standard. All countries of the world have their national flags, and since the end of the last war the number has greatly multiplied through the emergence of new states following the dissolution of the British and other empires. Unfortunately, some of these new states, like modern teenage children impatient to cast off all vestiges of parental authority, have not given much thought to the problem of replacing the former imperial blazon, but a number of former British colonies did have the good sense to consult the College of Arms with the result that the new national achievements and flags are very pleasing on both aesthetic and technical grounds.

It is not possible within the scope of a work such as this to describe and illustrate even the best of these new flags. We must in fact confine our attention to the Union Flag and Ensigns of Great Britain. And here it is necessary first to dispose of a popular misconception. The 'Union Jack' is not an heraldic combination of the national flags of the three kingdoms of England, Scotland and Ireland, because neither the Cross of St George, nor the Cross of St Andrew, nor the Cross of St Patrick was at any time the national arms of these countries respectively. The most that can be said is that they are the recognised emblems of the recognised patron saints of these countries, and when combined in the Union Flag provide the Sovereign with what Fox-Davies describes as 'the fighting emblem ... to be used by his soldiers or sailors for fighting purposes under certain specified circumstances'. It follows that this flag should never be flown by members of the general public. Apart from the military occasions mentioned above it can be flown only over a residence of the Sovereign when he or she is *not* in residence, or over a royal fortress or official residence of the Sovereign's representative. Against this may be set the reply of the then Home Secretary to a question asked in the House of Commons in 1933: 'The Union Flag is the national flag and may properly be flown by any British subject on land.' Such a statement conflicts with pronouncements of former Earls Marshal and the professional advice of the Kings of Arms; but so widespread is the custom of the flying of this flag by members of the general public on occasions of national rejoicing, that it seems more sensible to accept as lawful the official advice given to Parliament.

The Cross of St George St. George himself never had any connection with England. He was a Roman or Greek soldier in the service of the Emperor Diocletian, but received baptism as a Christian. According to the legend, he received martyrdom in the fourth century as the result of tearing down with his own hands the copy of the imperial edict of persecution which had been nailed to the door of the town hall of Nicomedia. After the triumph of Christianity in the reign of Constantine, the saint's cult spread rapidly in the East. How St George came to have associations with England can be briefly stated. According to a strongly entrenched legend, the saint with an army of angels came to the assistance of the hard-pressed Crusaders at Antioch during the First Crusade (1096-1099). King Richard I adopted the red cross of St George as a badge for his knights in the Third Crusade, and the subsequent popularity of this saint in England caused King Edward III to adopt him officially not only as England's national saint, but as the principal patron of his newly created Order of the Garter.

The Cross of St Andrew It is perhaps a matter of surprise that the Scots did not choose one of their great missionary saints as their patron, such as St Ninian or St Columba who have difinite historical associations with the country. It has never been seriously claimed that the apostle Andrew ever set foot in Scotland, of Caledonia, as the Romans of his day called it. Legend tells us that in the eighth century a stranger came to the Pictish King Aengus bearing some bones which he told the King were those of the apostle. The King believed this story, and gave permission for a church to enshrine the holy relics to be built at Kilrymont on the coast of Fifeshire. Centuries later a great cathedral replaced the old church, and pilgrims came from far and wide to acquire merit by prayer and offerings at the shrine of 'Scotland's Apostle'. At the end of the fifteenth century, at the request of King James IV, the Pope raised the See of St Andrew to the dignity of an archbishopric, the first Scotland ever had. According to a very ancient tradition the Apostle had suffered martyrdom for his faith by being crucified on a Roman cross in the form of a saltire. It was in the later Middle Ages that the white saltire on the blue field became recognised as the Banner of St Andrew and the national emblem.

The Cross of St Patrick Whereas this fourth-century saint, who was born in Wales, undoubtedly came to reside in Ireland and was personally responsible for the conversion to Christianity of many of the pagan chiefs and warriors, and became the patron saint of the country at a very early date, there is nothing to connect him with the red saltire on the white field which has become recognised as the Cross of St Patrick. In fact the first official recognition of this national banner seems to have been when it was produced to be incorporated in the National Flag following the Act of Union of 1801. St Patrick's saltire was made a principal motif of the insignia of the Illustrious Order of Saint Patrick,

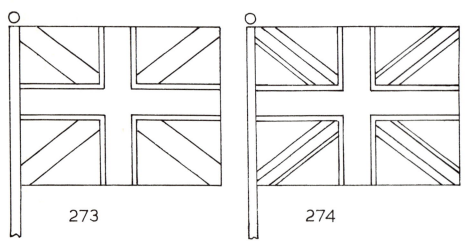

273   274

that Irish order of chivalry founded by King George III in 1785. The last surviving Knight Companion was the late Duke of Gloucester, who died in 1976. The Irish Republic has not adopted the red saltire as its national emblem.

The Union Flag Although the two kingdoms of England and Scotland came under one crown in 1603 with the accession of James VI to the English throne as James I, the Scots still kept their own Parliament and statute law. It was not until 1707 that Queen Anne's Act of Union abolished the Scottish legislature and transformed the English Parliament into the imperial Parliament of Great

Britain with Scottish representation in the House of Commons and representative Scottish peers sitting in the House of Lords. From that date until the union with Ireland in 1801 the national banner of Great Britain was a skilful combination of the banners of St George and St Andrew. (Fig 273). The Union Flag as we know it today can, therefore, be said to date from the very beginning of the nineteenth century. An important point to note is that, flown correctly, the *broad* white stripe which is the Cross of St Andrew must be on top at the corner nearest the head of the staff. The reason is that in the Union of the three kingdoms Scotland and St Andrew take precedence over Ireland and St Patrick. (Fig 274)

The Ensigns The White Ensign is a white flag charged with the Cross of St George, and bearing a reproduction of the Union Flag in the top quarter next to the staff. Its use is restricted to the Royal Navy and Royal Yacht Squadron. The Blue Ensign is a plain blue flag with the Union device in the top quarter next to the mast, in the form of a canton. It is a flag of the Royal Naval Reserve. The Red Ensign is similar to the Blue Ensign, except that the field is red. This is the flag flown at sea by all merchant ships and civilian craft entitled to fly British colours.

These three flags were called into being by royal warrants, and it is strictly illegal for them to be flown on land by other than official establishments of the three classes. Infringements of these rights at sea are subject to penalties in law.

The choice of the three field tinctures for these ensigns seems to have been dictated by the eighteenty-century naval custom of dividing the British fleet of ships of the line into three squadrons, each under the command of a Vice-Admiral, the White, Blue and Red, in that order of seniority.

Ecclesiastical Flags Most people in England are aware that on the great religious festivals it is customary for the flag of St George to be flown from the towers of English parish churches. What may not be so well known is a warrant issued in 1938 under the seal of the Earl Marshal which includes the following passage: 'the Banner or Flag proper to be flown upon any Church within the Provinces of Canterbury and York to be the Cross of Saint George and in the first quarter an escutcheon of the Arms of the See in which such Church is ecclesiastically situate'.

In spite of this ruling, it must be admitted that there are still very great number of parish churches of the Church of England that continue to fly the undifferenced flag of St George, and even, on national festivals, the Union Flag. As regards the former, one reason may well be that parish councils are reluctant to invest in the cost of an expensive new flag; and yet another that it is felt that the diocesan escutcheon confined to one quarter flying at a considerable height from the ground would be too small to be properly seen. In conclusion we might note that Westminster Abbey actually flies three flags or banners: (1) a banner emblazoned with the traditional arms of St Edward the Confessor, (2) a banner of St Peter, and (3) the differenced royal arms. The Abbey custom is to fly (1) on special festivals of the Abbey, (2) on great festivals of the universal Church, and (3) on the occasion of royal visits. It must be understood that the Abbey is a 'royal peculiar', and as such is specially privileged. Royal Peculiar is the official description of certain ecclesiastical buildings of the Church of England not subject to the ultimate authority of either diocesan bishop or archbishop of the province. The clergy of these establishments which include Westminster Abbey and the Chapels Royal enjoy their privileges by virtue of direct dependence on the monarch who is 'Supreme Governor of the Church'.

Index